ENDORSEMENTS

A testimony is a prophetic invitation into your own experience with God. I pray that as you read this book you too will encounter the heart of Jesus and receive your divine healing.

HEIDI BAKER, PhD
Founding Director, Iris Global

Hope is alive! If you are facing a mountain of hurt, this book relates a journey you too could take. The choice is yours. Choose life!

ROBIN SULLIVAN
On-Air Host of "The Praise Company"
Afternoon Drive DJ, 103.5FM WMUZ "The Light"
Detroit, Michigan

Hebrews 6:12 says, *"We do not want you to become lazy, but to imitate those who through faith and patience inherit what has been promised"* (NIV). Laura's testimony fully embodies this verse. Though she was diagnosed with a medically incurable disease many years ago, I have watched as she waits with expectation, full of faith, for the promise of God in her life. In *Even Though I Walk Through the Valley*, Laura, through her own story, teaches powerful principles about choosing life, even when situations look hopeless, and, through endurance, apprehending the promises of the Lord.

LOREN COVARRUBIAS
Senior Pastor, Mt. Zion Church
Clarkston, Michigan

When I sat down to read these pages, I didn't expect to find a true heroine who has lived through such difficult circumstances. I feel like my battle with cancer was nothing compared to what she has gone through. But her deep, rich treasures that she has found in her search and understanding of God's powerful promises makes me proud to say that she is my sister in the faith. She is a true godly hero. *"The godly people in the land are my true heroes..."* (Ps. 16:3 NLT).

KARYN BARRIGER
Co-Lead Pastor of Camino de Vida
Lima, Peru

A powerful work of ministry designed to permeate God's Word into our lives, *Even Though I Walk Through the Valley* encompasses God's faithfulness, grace, love, and His continual pursuit to see His people live in the fullness of His redemptive power. Laura speaks with such authority and passion. God has gifted us with such an anointed writer of today.

LINDSEY HUNTER
Former NBA point guard and two-time champion with the
Detroit Pistons and Los Angeles Lakers

It has been an honor beyond description to have known Laura the past two decades. She has been given access to a powerful grace, in spite of all the pain she endures daily, that is enabling her to stand strong in Jesus. In *Even Though I Walk Through the Valley*, Laura paves the way to this grace and shows us how to trust when it doesn't make sense and to believe when it seems impossible. I am personally indebted to Laura for showing me how to love and serve Jesus no matter what the circumstance and sacrifice.

JASON WHALEN
Senior Pastor, First Baptist Church of Elk Grove
Elk Grove, California

EVEN THOUGH
I WALK *through the*
VALLEY

DESTINY IMAGE₀ PUBLISHERS, INC.
P.O. Box 310, Shippensburg, PA 17257-0310
"Promoting Inspired Lives."

This book and all other Destiny Image, Revival Press, MercyPlace, Fresh Bread, Destiny Image Fiction, and Treasure House books are available at Christian bookstores and distributors worldwide.

For a U.S. bookstore nearest you, call 1-800-722-6774.
For more information on foreign distributors, call 717-532-3040.
Reach us on the Internet: www.destinyimage.com.

ISBN 13 TP: 978-0-7684-4211-3
ISBN 13 Ebook: 978-0-7684-8735-0

For Worldwide Distribution, Printed in the U.S.A.
1 2 3 4 5 6 7 8 / 17 16 15 14 13

EVEN THOUGH I WALK *through the* VALLEY

GOD'S HEALING POWER FOR RESTORATION & LOVE

LAURA M. KYMLA, M.A., L.P.C.

DEDICATION

To my husband Jerry, who has walked steadily with me, never wavering as he drew incredible strength in the Father's presence. Your consistent love and willingness to pour into each one of us brought predictability and peace to our home. No matter how weary you are, you have been there to listen, guide, and bring wisdom. When I could no longer stand, you held me and cried with me. When we needed a break from all of the trauma, you made us laugh. When we all share our feelings about who you are to this family, one common theme is apparent: You are a true warrior!

To my eldest daughter, Melissa, who works diligently to raise four children and provide support for a mother diagnosed with a chronic, serious illness. This is no small feat! When crisis hit, you came running, bringing a stable force to each situation. Whether it was hearing your comforting voice in an ambulance or allowing me to weep while you massaged my spine and ribs, you were not afraid to assist in any challenge put before you. Thank you for your gentle and patient care throughout the years and for the blessing of so many happy memories with Champ, Livia, Mia, and London. What a treasure lies within each one!

To Christopher, my son, who faced all the "giants" and incredible personal challenges during this crisis with the heart of the Father. Walking in true manhood, you never wavered in our darkest hours. You are always dependable, loving, and serving with an attitude of honor and gentleness, and I am privileged to call you *son*. You have become a true leader, willing to handle our personal affairs, as well as the very difficult details of my care in my weakest and most vulnerable moments.

To Carmen Rose, my daughter, who has cared for me with tenderness and strength while protecting my dignity with the fierceness of a mother bear. Surely, the truest sign of your sincerity and godly transparency is how you have conducted yourself in your private life. Your heart for people reflects God's Spirit within you, as you have shown true compassion through self-sacrifice. I will forever cherish every hospital stay with you sleeping next to me night after night. Though you must have wanted protection from the pain of all you heard and witnessed, you never left my side, facing this enemy without shrinking back. What a woman of grace and honor!

Jerry, Melissa, Christopher, and Carmen, I love you!

A SPECIAL ACKNOWLEDGMENT

Thanks to my dear sister, Ann Mauro-Vetter, graduate of the University of Notre Dame ('86). Your sensitivity and excellence in the editing of this book were a real gift to me. Your willingness to go before our Father in prayer when you needed guidance and your professionalism at every turn made it a joy to work with you. Thank you for turning this account of my journey into a written testimony of God's amazing faithfulness! My love always.

ACKNOWLEDGMENTS

To my pastors, Loren and Bonnie Covarrubias, "Mama" Jean Covarrubias, the staff of Mt. Zion, and our local church family: Your ministry, dedication, love, and prayers are treasures in our lives.

To my dear friends: Thank you for your unwavering love, intercession, and seasoned wisdom!

To my mom and dad and my sisters and brothers-in-law.

To Lindsey and Ivy Hunter and family. I love you!

To my dear aunts, Lois Serra and Clara Schmidt, for their prayer and support throughout the years, as well as their listening ears.

To my amazing team of doctors: Nicholas J. Gonzalez, M.D.; Kay Miller, M.D.; Dr. Sharon Havis; Kimberly Les, M.D.; Judie Goodman, D.O.; and to my incredible nurses for their support in allowing me to make decisions in my treatment, along with their guidance and sensitive care.

To the staff at Ed Fahey Associates Physical Therapy (including Ed Fahey and Sue Johnson, physical therapists, and Mrs. Sandy Hawthorne).

To my son-in-law, Bryan Nesbitt.

To Jamal Craft and Denise Cooley for their tremendous support in every way throughout this journey.

To Debbie Kelly for helping with the primary organization of the book material.

To Bret Autrey and Drew Neal for their prayers and consistent support.

To Pastor Bill Johnson, Bob Johnson, Mrs. Darliene Johnson, and the Bethel Church, Redding, California, family.

To Lisa Ott and our amazing team at Destiny Image Publishers.

To Jenni Kincaid for compiling and organizing the original manuscript.

My sisters and friends from *Our Lady Of The Lakes*, with whom I share forty-eight years of friendship: Sue Desmond Marshall, Erin Shaughnessy Asdell, and Annie Blust Romeo.

Every bone in my body laughing, singing,

"God, there's no one like You..."

(PSALM 35:10 MSG)

CONTENTS

INTRODUCTION

I WROTE THIS BOOK FOR YOU. THOUGH MY STORY IS AN ACCOUNT of a painful journey, it also testifies to God's intimate desire to demonstrate Himself to His people as Healer, Restorer, Deliverer, Provider, Shelter, and Father in the midst of a dark and devastating road. His loving interaction with me from the moment I was given the news of the seriousness of my physical condition opened up a whole new perspective of His love and of the word of hope He wanted to plant in me.

As the waves of crisis appeared endless, leaving my family barely able to walk with a sense of stability under our feet, it became very clear that we could not walk this journey alone. We soon found out that there was a community of believers ready to do what the Father asked of them, and in the process, be part of a powerful transformation, fresh anointing, and incredible outpouring of His Spirit. This story is proof of the power that exists when the "many-membered body" of Christ unites!

My prayer is that the Church walks in purity and power, emanating from a place of intimacy with His presence. It's *in* His presence that we are equipped to represent the *true* nature of our God. As our minds are renewed by the truth of His Word and the touch of His Spirit, we, His Church, will carry out our commission to *heal* the sick, *raise* the dead, and *preach* the good news of the Kingdom of God to the four corners of the earth.

As you read my journey, I believe it will encourage you to draw strength from the Lord in the secret place, no matter what you are going through in your life. As a professional counselor, I'll provide you with strategies to identify and defeat personal battles over issues such as condemnation, shame, fear, guilt, hopelessness, and despair. I trust that these principles will inspire you to stay focused on God's goodness and faithfulness, fully confident in the rich promises won for you through Jesus' sacrifice at the cross. At the end of each chapter, I will pose reflection questions that will encourage you to search your heart before the Lord and apply the principles to your own life. Like me, *you will* overcome every "giant" in your life that attempts to steal, destroy, kill, and rob you of your inheritance in Jesus' name!

May you be strengthened and equipped as a member of the mighty army of God in this, the Church's finest hour!

Laura M. Kymla, M.A., L.P.C.

Chapter 1

THE JOURNEY BEGINS

*But if we hope for what is still unseen by us, we wait
for it with patience and composure* (Romans 8:25).

It was the summer of 1994, and in the upper Midwest, we
long for the summer months! Through the dark and cold of winter, we lie in wait for the renewed energy, new life, and hope that
come with the summer sun. With no reason to expect anything
different that year, I went about my work as Bereavement Coor-
dinator for a local hospice program. At the age of thirty-seven, I
was an active wife, mother, and business professional. However,
I began to experience unusual symptoms of exhaustion and pro-
fuse night sweats. At the insistence of friends and family, I sought
out the consultation of an internist. Now, going to the doctor
for anything took a bit of persuading, especially because I spent
most of my workday counseling terminally ill patients and their
families. Succumbing to the pleas of my loved ones, I made an
appointment to have blood work done. After a couple weeks and

no response, I assumed everything was fine. However, one day, while I was facilitating a children's grief support group, my receptionist knocked at the door and interrupted, "Laura, you have an urgent call."

I asked my assistant to take over the session. As I picked up the receiver, I was in sheer disbelief at what I heard. Apparently, my blood test results were pointing to some form of cancer, and I was instructed to meet my doctor at the hospital for further testing. In shock, I informed my director that I had to leave work immediately. Seeing that I was visibly shaken, she paged my husband and arranged to have a co-worker drive me to the hospital. Little did I realize the journey that lay ahead—a journey that would turn a season of light into a winter of dark despair.

The test results showed signs of multiple myeloma, an incurable cancer found in the bone marrow. An appointment was made with a local oncologist for bone marrow aspiration. The diagnosis confirmed indolent myeloma. Shortly after, I was referred to the head doctor of bone marrow at a large hospital in Detroit. Because the results showed the cancer in an early stage, I was convinced there was a mistake. My husband Jerry and I went to the cancer hospital alone, as we could not have imagined the report we were about to receive. I felt a sense of darkness as we walked into the bone marrow unit.

The doctor reviewed my file, and more blood work was drawn. With tears in his eyes, he shared that the doctors would do all they could to help me, but the prognosis was not good. "I know you probably feel relatively good at this time," he hesitated, "but this disease will progress. Myeloma, which is usually more aggressive in young people, is so rare; we do not have much experience to draw on. We will monitor the progression monthly and perform a bone marrow transplant at the end of stage one or early stage two. If you survive the transplant, we will only be able to buy you time. How much time is questionable, as you are very young. I am so sorry."

Buy me time? His words brought a threatening torrent of emotions. He continued as I wept in disbelief, "Do you have any siblings? We would like to type them in order to find a donor right away so we are prepared when the time comes. Did your mother have a garden in which she used pesticides?" My head was swimming in a sea of my own questions as I attempted to answer his.

"You say this is incurable. Do you know of any other doctors in the nation who have had success treating this type of cancer?"

He replied, "None."

Jerry and I hung on to each other as we left the examining room, walking down endless hallways of tile and "institution" green walls. Battered by the news, Jerry fought to maintain his composure while driving home. We pulled off the expressway several times, attempting to steady ourselves before arriving at a restaurant to talk things over together. *How would we possibly report the news to our family and friends?*

The events that took place from this point on were unbelievable. What should have been a time of drawing strength and courage from loved ones turned into a nightmare. A well-known cliché states, "Freedom is never free." I had no idea that the journey I was about to take would cost me everything. The battle I was about to fight was more about inner healing than physical healing, and the battle began with my extended family.

I grew up in a large Italian family with seven sisters. My mother was born in Italy, and my father, also a full-blooded Italian, was born in the United States. His parents lived in the same southern Italian town as my mother's family and migrated to St.

Paul, Minnesota, for a better life before he and his three siblings were born. My mom came to America at the age of eight to live with her father and brother, who left Italy years prior to prepare the way for the rest of her family. My father grew up in Illinois, and after graduating from the University of Notre Dame, he worked his entire career at General Motors. While raising all of us, my father took a second job as a night janitor at the local Catholic church and school, which my sisters and I attended for both elementary and high school. Raising eight girls did not come naturally to my father. His own mother died tragically when he was only thirteen, leaving him in the care of his father. Losing his mother during the vulnerable teen years deeply affected my dad, and his own father—a cold and insensitive man—was hardly a substitute for a mother's loving tenderness. Consequently, my dad raised us with an iron rod, teaching us to live a life of discipline and obedience.

Where did I fit in? As number six out of eight daughters, I was the people pleaser and the approval seeker. There was a lot of competition among my siblings for my father's approval. Passive and walking in shame, I constantly looked to my older sisters for my value and significance. This behavior was reinforced in Catholic school, as I was a model child who was always willing to do whatever it took to stand out and be special. If I failed at something, I hid in embarrassment. These unhealthy patterns of behavior affected all of us, and they would soon impact my family's reaction to my diagnosis and treatment choices.

I'm sure many of you can relate to an upbringing that is similar to mine, having grown up without a healthy sense of personal worth and value. Instead, we learned in a performance-based environment where "right" behavior dictated the measure of love and approval we received from those closest to us, our parents. In a sense, if we didn't "perform" well, we were not loved. As Christians, we must receive the revelation that our heavenly Father chose us and loves us, not because of our "right behavior," but because of who we are through His Son. Jesus paid the price for our freedom from fear, guilt, shame, hopelessness, and insecurity. Every day, you should confidently declare over your life, "I am loved. I am accepted. I am secure and confident in who I am because of my Father's great love."

Meanwhile, in our quest to learn more about my illness, Jerry began to research alternative methods for the treatment of incurable disease, as well as studying the medical books for any conclusive information about myeloma. Because Jerry's job consisted of spending time with psychiatric patients in hospitals, more information was available to him than what was typically found at public libraries.

The consensus was that the progression of myeloma was unpredictable to say the least, and once lesions formed on the bones, my chance for long-term survival was poor. Jerry's research led him to Nicholas Gonzalez, M.D., a classically trained immunologist in New York City who was successfully treating patients with many types of cancer, giving them extended life quality with proteolytic enzyme therapy. After listening to Dr. Gonzalez speak on tape at a medical convention, we knew this was the treatment to pursue. I was too young to "buy time." Instead, I wanted to *live*—to embrace a full and active life while raising my then eleven-year-old son Christopher and my seven-year-old daughter Carmen.

Obviously, alternative medicine was not respected back then, and insurance carriers were not willing to pay for it. Jerry quickly put our new home on the market, and we moved to a smaller, older home within seven months of my diagnosis. Jerry found a second job working as a counselor in a large agency, and we began our quest for my admittance into Dr. Gonzalez's program. In shock for the better part of that year, my emotions ranged between hysteria, fear, disbelief, and denial. I was grieving the loss of my home in the country, which I loved so dearly, my hospice career, to which I could not emotionally give my all while preparing to battle cancer myself, and my health. Once accepted into Dr. Gonzalez's program, I began an aggressive protocol of detoxification, supplementation (200 pills per day), and a specialized organic diet.

During a quick visit to our pastor's office, he revealed a surprise to me when he said, "Laura, set the cancer aside at this moment. God is doing a greater work in you. What you need to be delivered from is the need for approval." His words resonated in my spirit. *Deliver me, Lord, that I may be healed!*

Meanwhile, my immediate family members were facing their own struggles. My battle became theirs. Exhausted but determined, I did my best to help my children adjust to their new environment and encourage them in the midst of great loss, while constantly feeling ill for the first few years of my treatment. Jerry was now working all day and did not return home until ten o'clock in the evening from his second counseling position. It took every ounce of effort to put one foot in front of the other, a feat that would not have been possible without the support of our local church. I knew I could not walk this road without counsel for my family and myself. There were days when I fell to the floor in grief, and no words could describe what I felt in that place of brokenness. Groans of pain would come forth from the deepest part of my spirit. I did not know how to possibly pray in my pain. My pastor told me to just start there—right in that place of brokenness and despair. "Let God take your pain, Laura. If that is what is in you, then He will receive your wailing." *Take what I have to offer, Lord, and make it holy in Your sight.*

When I share my experiences with others, I always tell them that I spent more time on the floor than standing for a long time. It seemed I had spent my whole professional career learning to help people in their grief, and yet, I could not help myself in my pain. I read once that every person goes through a "dark night of the soul." Clearly, this was mine. How could I trust God to protect and deliver me when I never grew to trust others? In my formative years, those closest to me often exposed my wounds rather than covering me, often shaming and accusing rather than loving me. How would they handle this diagnosis of "weakness" and "need" called cancer?

Multiple myeloma is an extremely rare cancer, which resulted in a lot of confusion and questions from some extended family members. My choice of treatment was seen as "unnecessary," and now, the fact that I was no longer a Catholic after fourteen years was a problem that permeated every interaction, every conversation. Somehow the crisis of my diagnosis opened the door to all the disappointment and issues that my father had buried for years. Every aspect of my life was now in question; I felt exposed at the very core of my being.

One might ask why a loving God would seemingly "allow" such pain and destruction, as my life seemed shattered with no hope of recovery. These events forced me to come face-to-face with God. Somewhere in the midst of contending with Him and taking a hard look at my past and what was left of me, I found that God was lovingly orchestrating my liberation. I began to study boundaries in relationships, forgiveness, moving on, and many other topics pertaining to personal and spiritual growth. Clearly, I would have to invest in my healing process.

I want to clarify for you that by "investing in my healing process," I'm not in any way implying that I need to *earn* healing. The finished work of Jesus on the cross was enough payment for that. There is nothing to be *earned*. Instead, in co-laboring with the Father through study of the Word, regular time in His presence, and godly counsel (the *investment*), destructive "roots" from the past are uncovered and healed. The process I have just described is a step toward the prosperity of soul described in Third John 2. Do you know that God desires the same for you? If you have unresolved hurt or brokenness from your past, today is your day to begin the healing process. Search out promises in the Word that address your need. Write them down. Meditate on them daily. Declare them out loud over your life. Read great books and listen to sermons that minister life to you.

Seek godly counsel, and most of all, expect the Lord to transform your life.

Having been in the counseling field for a number of years, I declared boldly that I was finished with helping people, at least in the clinical ways to which I was accustomed. Given my circumstances, I would focus on taking care of myself, at least for the near future. So many wonderful people came into my life to bring words of encouragement and hope. The Bible tells us, *"The tongue has the power of life and death..."* (Prov. 18:21 NIV). How I needed those healing words that would bring life and health to my bones! In time, a supportive network of faithful friends gathered near to keep me pressing forward. One by one, a number of my extended family members came to my aid, as well. Since these relationships have been restored over time, I am now able to freely give aid and support to my parents when needed, while maintaining a clear separation between *who I am* and *what they believe*.

Many other events happened after this period that "grew me up," and by trusting again, I slowly agreed to counsel a few people out of my home and allow others into my life. What began as rubble turned into a larger counseling practice that Jerry and I shared, which has helped hundreds of people heal their marriages, overcome addictions, and conquer the effects of abuse. We were often asked to speak at marriage retreats and men's and women's breakfasts, which gave us an opportunity to give back to others in their desperation—to draw from the well of our experience and offer refreshment.

You might be facing a tumultuous situation in your own life. It is in this place that you have to "dig your heels in" and trust your Father with complete abandon. You can trust Him because He loves you! Let the words of the Hebrew writer be as much comfort to you as they are to me: *"I will not in any way fail you nor give you up nor leave you without support. [I will] not, [I will] not, [I will] not in any degree leave you helpless nor forsake nor let [you] down (relax My hold on you)! [Assuredly not!]"* (Heb. 13:5). What a promise we have in Christ, even in the midst of the storm!

As we struggled to regain our focus and some sense of normalcy, we faced many unexpected challenges along the way. An attempt at using my husband's released retirement money to remodel the main floor of our home turned into another disaster, as his life savings were stolen when the builder filed bankruptcy and left the state. After getting legal help, the attorney general's office worked with us to pay off the subcontractors. A miracle brought many wonderful men from our church to volunteer their time and finish the work after our home was left with drywall hanging and electrical wires exposed. I cooked on an electric burner in my basement and slept and counseled out of our bedroom for the better part of a year. What could have possibly been accomplished through this mess? Relationships were built that would have never formed any other way, and a support group was developed for the young married couples involved in our practice. Most significantly, we developed a relationship with Melissa, a young adult who came from a life of abuse and alcoholism. Melissa never knew what it was like to be a part of a healthy, loving family, but she was soon to find out! After we offered Melissa many years of "spiritual parenthood," she became our beautiful, adopted daughter in 2004. We are now the proud in-laws of her husband, Bryan, and the grandparents of their four beautiful children.

One year later, in 2005, upon recommendation of an orthopedic surgeon, I had an abdominoplasty to repair a five-inch tear in my abdominal wall. Providing correct support in my core would help prevent further damage to a 75-degree hyperlordotic curvature of the spine. After surgery and countless prayers, the spine miraculously straightened far beyond everyone's expectations! I had been born with a deformity in my sacral spine (a genetic defect), and for the first time in years, I was pain-free and felt as though I was given a new start in life. A new x-ray proved that my spine was now normal, and the horizontal sacrum was in the correct position. One doctor, while comparing the old x-ray to the new, stated that the change was not possible at the hands of a physician.

I was very athletic all of my life and was working hard to get back into good shape while following my enzyme therapy program. I was never happier! Jerry and I took our first week-long vacation in eleven years to Bar Harbor, Maine, and the opportunity to get away alone was refreshing. Connecting and laughing together for this length of time was something we had not experienced in many years since Jerry's job and our counseling practice kept us working from morning until late in the evening and on weekends.

We returned home from our vacation to face a new phase of life. We were busy, but it felt good to have a sense of normalcy again, and our expectations for many good days ahead were rekindled. Sadly, our hopes were cut short one September afternoon in 2005. While I was opening the door to let our dogs play in the yard, a bee flew into the kitchen and dove straight at me. Being allergic to bees, I grabbed a fly swatter, lifted my knee on the counter, and swung into the kitchen window to kill it. As popping sounds erupted from my spine, I let out a cry and dropped to the floor in pain.

Boldly attempting to move about my kitchen in the usual manner, I buckled over in pain, clinging to the counter. The phone rang. *How could she have known?* In that very moment, my daughter, Carmen, just happened to call home between classes at college. Responding quickly to my need, she contacted my son, Christopher, who arrived immediately with my pastor's wife, Bonnie, and my good friend, Nita. Bonnie prayed with me before they assisted me into the car and drove to the doctor's office. *Thank You, Lord, for that deep connection from my very core to the hearts of my sweet children!*

Within four weeks of that incident, my back went into severe spasms, and I was unable to move in any direction without pain. Realizing that I needed more specialized assistance, I went to my surgeon, and he diagnosed me with severely strained discs in the lumbar region of my spine. Complete bed rest, muscle relaxers, and something for pain were prescribed. Although there was improvement, becoming active again caused more problems.

Seven months passed, and there were more bad days than good. The spasms began again, and a new bulging disc in the thoracic area of the spine proved a setback. The nights were tortuous and long, bringing a level of pain I had never known. I experienced a roller coaster of emotions and felt trapped in a prison of pain. Most of my days were spent in bed or in a chair, as

I tried to believe again for healing. Like the father of the demon-possessed boy, I cried, "Lord, I believe, help me in my unbelief!" (See Mark 9:24.)

With prayer, support, and help from family and friends, I learned to surrender to the process while continuing to hope. Though discouraged by the physical challenges, I became strong enough to stand amidst the storm. Even though I was afraid at times, I knew in my heart that a marvelous birthing was about to take place. Though tears flowed from the pain, they brought baptism to a new sense of self. I pressed on, waiting for another miracle.

Like me, many of you have experienced seasons of tremendous "ups and downs" where it seemed as though everything was out of control and heading down a disastrous path. I've learned that in these times, in the midst of the trial and battle, we have to strengthen ourselves in the Lord as the psalmist did. Psalm 46:1-5 declares:

> *God is our Refuge and Strength [mighty and impenetrable to temptation], a very present and well-proved help in trouble. Therefore we will not fear, though the earth should change and though the mountains be shaken into the midst of the seas, though its waters roar and foam, though the mountains tremble at its swelling and tumult. Selah [pause, and calmly think of that]! There is a river whose streams shall make glad the city of God, the*

holy place of the tabernacles of the Most High. God is in the midst of her, she shall not be moved; God will help her right early [at the dawn of the morning].

When the trials of life are staring you in the face and when situations look hopeless, will you fix your eyes on Jesus? Think of a difficult circumstance that you have recently encountered. Take a moment to still your heart and pray, "Father, I feel like I'm in over my head. I know You hear me when I pray. I ask for a greater measure of peace and confidence in You in this situation. I declare that You are my help today. I declare the promise that Your thoughts and plans for me are for good. I declare that You are working on my behalf even when I can't see it with my natural eyes. I receive Your love and thank You for victory in Jesus' name." Keep your eyes fixed on Him. Trust me, He'll never, ever let You out of His grip.

Chapter 2

AN UNEXPECTED REALITY

Then called I upon the name of the Lord: O
Lord, I beseech You, save my life and deliver me!
Gracious is the Lord, and [rigidly] righteous; yes,
our God is merciful. The Lord preserves the simple;
I was brought low, and He helped and saved me.
Return to your rest, O my soul, for the Lord has
dealt bountifully with you (Psalm 116:4-7).

IT WAS MAY 1, 2006—ABOUT SIX MONTHS AFTER MY BACK INJURY
and twelve years since my initial diagnosis. I knew I was progres-
sively getting worse when I observed the concern in my friends'
eyes as I entered my kitchen to thank them for all they had done.
Two of my close friends had been at my house all day, cleaning
and organizing a home that needed much tender care. So many
activities that were a natural part of my routine as a wife and

mother were left undone; the pain had stolen them, one by one. The following day, after I experienced a very painful weekend, the house seemed dead without the sound of my friends' energetic voices directing one another in their plan to help me. The quiet was now deafening as I picked up the phone and called my friend, Marilyn, to talk. "Marilyn, I'm in trouble." I could barely speak the pain was so intense.

"What do you mean?" she retorted. I could sense the fear in my friend's voice while I explained the agony I was experiencing. Marilyn did her best to comfort me and reassured me of her prayers. She insisted I call her as soon as I heard from my orthopedic surgeon regarding the MRI that was performed that morning.

After ending my phone call with Marilyn, I recalled the excellent report I had received from Dr. Gonzalez just seven months earlier. After that appointment, my sister, Roseanne, planned a Thanksgiving celebration to allow me an opportunity for reconciliation with my parents after having been estranged from them for a period of time. Gathered together at the dinner table, each person drew a name and was asked to prepare a verbal blessing over one another. Desiring restoration with my mom and dad, I had prepared a blessing to speak over my father as well. Not knowing my father had drawn my name, I was left unprepared for his plan to open fire with words of disappointment and disgust. Again, my decision to leave the Catholic Church was at the core of his berating. The room was silent as my husband, children, and sisters, Roseanne and Barbara, and brother-in-law, Jim, went into shock. Jerry grieved that encounter, and in prayer, he made the decision that my father was not ready for relationship. My hopes for restoration were sadly dashed, and I was left to enter another season of grief and loss.

L ooking back on this situation, I see that there was a root of rejection in my life that desperately needed healing. Negative words are powerful weapons that can pierce the deepest part of our beings. They are most damaging when they come from someone who has intimate access to our hearts, especially a parent. Proverbs 18:21 makes it clear that *"Death and life are in the power of the tongue…"* Certainly, this was the case for me, as feelings of brokenness and condemnation spilled over into my daily life because of my father's verbal abuse. Such moments when our very character is battered and belittled, are all too familiar to many. As we process through such events, however, we have two options: sink into depression and defeat or actively seek healing for our broken spirits and wounded souls. In order to finally defeat this "giant" in my life, I understood that I had to *live* the principles I had taught so many people throughout my years as a professional counselor. For years, my worth and value as a person were dependent upon my performance. This mindset, stemming from brokenness, fed a dysfunctional pattern of approval addiction. Identifying (and taking time to work through) areas of brokenness with a trusted counselor or pastor is an important step to victory in this area.

I spent the day resting and praying until the phone rang; I could see it was my doctor calling after office hours. "Laura, I am reading your report from your MRI, and I don't know how to say this to you. Your spine is full of bone marrow disease, and you need an oncologist right away. I have already called one on your behalf, and I would like you to contact him and set up an appointment immediately."

I was stunned and immediately picked up the phone to call my husband, Jerry. From deep within, a guttural scream poured forth, "Oh my God! I am full of cancer!"

Jerry, stunned, began to cry out himself, "Don't leave me, Laura! I can't live without you...Please stay on the phone with me until I get to you!"

I could not think straight, but one thing I knew: I needed to call the church. My pastors had walked this road with me for twelve years since my initial diagnosis in 1994, and I knew I could not handle this news alone, so I assured Jerry that I would call him back. I could barely talk as the church receptionist answered the phone. Sensing the urgency of the situation, she immediately connected me with the pastor, who was on call that evening. When he answered the phone, I began to scream, "Dave, I am full of cancer...How am I going to tell the kids?"

Nothing can prepare a mother to share such a harsh reality with her children. After all, we had been through so much already, and I felt that this latest news would pierce their hearts.

How can they possibly walk this road with me, their mother? Oh, Father, please spare us this road!

Dave immediately prayed for me and reassured me that God had not abandoned me. He truly believed that there was a bigger purpose for this new valley and that God would walk through it with me. A peace came over me long enough to make more phone calls. Hearing Marilyn's voice brought the safety of expressing my grief, and she let me know she was on her way immediately. One by one, my dear friends and family came and encircled Jerry, Christopher, Carmen, and me. There was a quiet but powerful presence of the Holy Spirit as each one came and sat. I could barely speak. My thoughts were scattered. I kept combing the room for my children, as they could not sit still. Christopher went into the yard to be alone after I shared the news, and he had not yet returned to the house. He was too grief-stricken to speak to anyone. *Oh Lord, help my children; someone come and help my children.*

Hours passed, and I was still sitting on the couch, numb and lost in my fear and grief. Every bone in my body ached; it had been difficult to move around freely for months. I was aware of Jerry sitting very close to me, at times weeping, burying his head in his hands in despair. He had to leave the room occasionally, but his good friends remained faithfully at his side and prayed, bringing the sweet communion of the presence of the Lord in our midst. With each passing hour, more close friends gathered, one by one, in a circle of life-giving strength. They surrounded us in prayerful silence as each brought words of life. Before I knew it, my pastor's mother, Jean Covarrubias ("Mama Jean," as we call her) was standing over me anointing my forehead with oil and speaking life to me.

"Laura," she spoke softly as my eyes followed her like a scared child searching for her mother, "Don't worry about what to pray or how to pray at this time. The Body of Christ will bring you before the Lord, and we will carry you. Just rest now." She encouraged me to call her any time, day or night, and reminded me that my name would be placed in the petition basket at the miracle service each Tuesday.

I heard the door open again, and instant relief fell over me as my pastors, Loren and Bonnie Covarrubias, walked into the room. Loren had encouraged me in my walk with the Lord throughout all of our years at Mt. Zion. His wife, Bonnie, herself a cancer survivor, knew the pain of hearing those words from a doctor. We talked about many things that evening as they both brought such a peace and comfort to our whole family. It is amazing how faith can be stirred by the presence of our family in Christ; spirit-to-spirit, we were all able to touch one another that evening as we clung together in search of hope unseen.

Despite the shock and numb disbelief swirling within me, I watched with a mother's eyes as Pastor Loren went outside to speak with Christopher. Having worked at the church since he was a young boy, Christopher was now finishing college and preparing for a call to full-time ministry. He trusted Pastor Loren and was able to pour out his heart to him. Somehow, the shock of my original diagnosis years before had forced Christopher to bury his emotions deep within, but they came rushing forth in the presence of our trusted pastor. *Thank You, Lord, for sending help. Please help my son. Give strength to his spirit; calm his fears.*

Carmen, typical of her energetic, vibrant nature, immediately called her big sister, Melissa, who was living in Germany at the time with her husband, Bryan. With the unshakeable determination that our eldest daughter has always possessed, Melissa quickly made arrangements for the care of her four children, and with the loving support of our son-in-law, she was on a plane the next day headed for home.

The following morning brought anxiety as I opened my eyes and prayed for the courage to confront the day. Carmen's compassionate face was in mine when I opened my eyes. "Mom, I'll help you get out of bed. Here are your enzymes." By this time, I was no longer able to lift my pitcher of water or walk with a glass in my hand. Everything had to be brought to me like a child. *But, Lord, it is I who should be taking care of them!*

Melissa would arrive home that same day; how I grieved the thought of not greeting her in my usual manner. It was part of my nature to prepare all of her favorite desserts and meals whenever she came home. Melissa came into this world surrounded by alcohol and drug use. She was the victim of much neglect on many levels, and my heart ached for our dear adopted daughter. What would this do to her? I wanted to provide for her a warm environment and let her feel the love and restorative power of the Father.

Usually the one to take care of others in need, I would have to surrender to the care of so many in the days ahead. Melissa came home ready to care for me and did so with much energy and tenderness. She would not hear anyone speak death regarding my condition and, together with Carmen, fought to preserve my dignity and peace throughout the beginning stages of my treatment. Good news was expressed in so many ways, extending life to my spirit as my body slowly began to weaken with each passing day. *How precious are the feet of those that bring good news!*

We all walked slowly into the doctor's office to meet my oncologist. This was a visit I never wanted to experience, and my mind was foggy as my family helped me into the examining room. I was very unsure of what to expect, as I had been under the care of Dr. Gonzalez, one of the top alternative medical doctors in the world.

At the time of my diagnosis twelve years prior, the only recommended treatment for myeloma was a bone marrow transplant. The chance of survival was only 50 percent during the procedure, not including the high risk of infection and other diseases, as well as the risk of post-transplant rejection. Knowing that a transplant early on in the disease process would shorten my lifespan considerably, my husband Jerry began to search medical journals for someone, somewhere, who was treating rare cancers with success. Multiple myeloma has remained an incurable disease, so educating ourselves to the reality of treatments available and their impact on the overall lifespan of the patient was paramount to our plan of action. We immediately began to pray for the Lord to lead us in our search, and our number one request was that He would grant us the privilege of being treated by a Christian doctor. At that time, I was only thirty-seven years old, and as a young mother, I intended to do everything I could to ensure that I would see my children reach adulthood and beyond. Within six months of beginning Dr. Gonzalez's proteolytic enzyme therapy program, my night sweats and fatigue began to dissipate. Given all these considerations, so many questions raced through my mind as we waited for the oncologist to arrive. *How could things have gone so wrong in my treatment? What are we going to do?* There was so much to know and understand. Sensing the weight of it all, I breathed in deeply as the doctor entered the room. *Lord, grant me Your peace, which surpasses all human understanding.*

The oncologist walked in, picked up the phone in the office, and ordered, "Get Dr. Gonzalez on the phone, please." Looking back at me, he continued, "We are not going to break up a twelve-year relationship here, and I know you want to speak with him." He quickly assessed my condition while speaking with Dr. Gonzalez, and both concurred that chemotherapy was needed. Immediately, I trusted the wisdom of this stranger since he was willing to go to such lengths to make me feel safe in his care. Through a haze of fear, knowing I was about to embark upon an unknown journey, I surrendered in my weakness to the plan.

Our son, Christopher, looked at the doctor and asked, "Are you going to help my mom?"

The doctor replied, "We will help her," and then he calmly asked everyone but Jerry and me to leave the room.

I was in too much pain to worry about what was going to come out of this man's mouth. "We have to move quickly. I want her at the hospital as soon as we can get her scheduled for a biopsy, and we must begin chemotherapy immediately."

Even to this day, the oncologist, who we affectionately call "Doc," often reminds me of my condition at that first meeting; "You were not able to walk well and could not even sit on the examining table without help." It is remarkable to me that the peaks and valleys experienced while fighting a terminal illness become jumbled together in my memory. *Lord, on the other side of this tangled web of emotions, I know that You will reveal a beautiful tapestry of hope and rebirth.*

Jerry and the kids left the office to handle things at home as Jerry had to prepare his staff at work for a scheduled upcoming conference in Chicago. I knew all of them were struggling through the motions of life while trying to cope with the pangs of shock that washed over them throughout the day. I tried to encourage everyone to take one minute at a time and trust the Lord. I was overwhelmed by the comfort we received at the hands of our loved ones.

From that meeting, my friend Nita walked me down the hall to radiology for a total body scan. As she helped me into the restroom before my x-rays, I threw my arms around her neck and screamed, "I never wanted to go down this road. Oh, God, please don't make me go down this road!" I knew I could grieve with Nita since she had been taking me to my doctor appointments for my back pain, and she herself was a cancer survivor. She knew what it was like to fight for her life.

Nita helped me get undressed and graciously climbed onto the x-ray table with me, literally sliding half of her upper body under my spine so I could lay my body, racked with pain and broken bones, onto the table. What courage and love emanated from her eyes as I screamed in agony, "Please don't leave me, Nita!"

Her words softly reassured me, "I am not going anywhere."

As I lay waiting for the technician to begin, I heard in my spirit a word Pastor Loren had spoken in prayer over me three years earlier. "Deep calls unto deep, daughter; the Lord is taking you to a deeper place in Him so you can go to a deep place with others." My heart melted as the Holy Spirit recalled the prophetic word that was coming to fruition and preparing me for this journey. By now I had learned, not just heard, that *My thoughts are not your thoughts, neither are your ways My ways, says the Lord*" (Isa. 55:8). Over the years of my walk with Him, the Lord had worked in my spirit that I must "count the cost" of my calling. My thoughts were racing between the fear of dying and the pulling of the Lord to trust Him, as He promised victory and healing in His Word. How I loved the sweet sound of His voice, and I clung to every word that proceeded from His mouth, for it was my sustenance—my very breath.

Being able to recount the Lord's faithfulness over my life brought the security of knowing He would hold my hand through this valley. Had I not learned that God takes us *through* painful circumstances, not *around* them, in order to produce in us the fruit of the Spirit? I recalled a conversation I had with the Lord a couple of years before on a walk. I was praying and said to the Lord, "Father, I want to walk in Your power." He answered, "Purity is power, daughter. I am not talking about sexual purity or other ways your natural mind would think; I am talking about being one with Me. Purity is being able to walk in My way of thinking and doing. When you learn of My ways, then you will walk in My power." I have never forgotten those words and have ministered to many from that revelation. With greater clarity, I could now see in the natural how the Word working in us is a double-edged sword. It was now cutting into my spirit deeper than it had ever cut before.

I was becoming keenly aware of how every revelation brings us more intimately into relationship with the Lord. His visitation is a fire that burns away everything that binds us—everything that would hold us back from receiving the true liberty that He died to give us. The freedom is not just for us individually, but a spirit of liberty is destined to be poured out on all flesh for the plans and purposes of His Kingdom. Each time He has taken me to a deeper place in Him, He shows me my heart of unbelief. Would I trust Him to complete the work He had begun in me? Would I believe that He would be faithful to the promise He made to me just two years before?

As I began this dreaded and uncertain path, the sweet breath of His Spirit harmoniously and rhythmically echoed, "Behold, I make all things new." Surely, this was a declaration that Jesus made about His ability and desire to restore us. As I stared at my body, the large tumors pushing through my ribs, sternum, and side were more evidence of the making of a prison door than of new life. *What in the world are You doing here, Lord?* The pain in my spine and pelvis was so intense I began hallucinating.

One night in May 2006, Jerry found me crawling around my bed in a state of panic. Waves of terror crashed in and around me; I could hear their roar and see them like a tsunami in the eyes of my husband and children. *Oh Father, hold tightly to me as I cannot bear to look up at the violent destruction around me!*

After a terrible night of hallucinations, the next morning led me down a long, uncertain path as I walked the hallway to the chemotherapy room for blood work and Zometa, an I.V. bone strengthener. It was difficult for the nurse to hit my vein, and she suggested we return after my biopsy and try again. My frustration mounted. Nita was faithfully at my side yet again, and I begged her to come close to me in that moment. She gave me a questioning look. I pleaded with her again to draw near and threw my arms around her neck for support. With all of the protection of a mother bear, Nita strongly encouraged the nurse and said, "Do it now!" I hated being in that chair. I hated that room! I gained my composure, and thankfully the nurse found the vein. I just wanted to leave and never return. I wanted my life back and did not want to accept the new life awaiting me. *Lord, it is a painful road this dying to self.*

Nita brought me home and began to busy herself in my kitchen, while Jerry helped me into my pajamas. As he bent over to dress me, I clung to his neck, and together we wailed as he tried to hold me up. "I know, oh God, I know," Jerry cried, "I wish I could take this from you!" I saw Nita peek around the corner and quietly head back down the stairs. She had obviously heard our screams and wanted to make sure I had not fallen. Recognizing and knowing this scene all too well, Nita knew she was standing on sacred ground. The delicate process of breaking was beginning, and the fire—so intensely hot—could not touch us, for the Spirit surrounded us like a shield. I needed to get some rest. *Not again, Lord, please do not take me to this dark place.*

Providing a welcome respite, Dave, a minister from the church, arrived to give our family communion. Our visit was life-giving as we all gathered around in our living room. Dave shared with us that the Lord had reminded him about the five smooth stones that David washed in the brook as he prepared to defeat Goliath. "There are five of you, and each one will lift up and bring strength to the rest when they are weary." The kids presented me with new running shoes to symbolically represent my running toward the goal of healing. My heart grieved the loss of my athletic ability as I lifted the shoes out of the box—one more part of me broken and outpoured for purposes yet unknown. I swallowed hard as I thanked the kids for the thoughtful gift. Their gift spoke volumes about their hopes and dreams for me, and I knew I needed to respond to them carefully. I could hardly speak, but promised I would fight for life. The message Dave brought to us would be confirmed in the coming months. We began preparing for this fight in the presence of the Lord by receiving the sacrament of communion. We believed in the healing power of communion, and with faith in the finished work on the cross, we confessed our frailty and our need for the Lord's strength, wisdom, and power to heal.

Every hour brought new challenges for all of us—emotional, physical, and spiritual challenges. That evening our spiritual son and daughter, Lindsey and Ivy, came as soon as they could to help, while Jerry worked in our counseling practice downstairs. Lindsey, a point guard for the Detroit Pistons, knew how to motivate someone in the heat of a battle. Holding my hand, he just sat quietly at my side and listened as each of my children expressed anger, sadness, and grief at the state of my health. I shared with them that I, too, was confused and felt betrayed since Jerry (who they affectionately call "Papa") and I had finally reached a place in our lives where we were discussing plans for our latter years together. We began to dream about the places we wanted to see and the call of God on our lives.

It was difficult and painful to share these shattered hopes with the kids, but Jerry and I had always believed in allowing them to ask questions regarding any obstacle we faced so we could provide them with the security and hope they needed in the Word of God. We did not want them to think they had to protect me from their grief, as my biggest concern was their carrying an emotional load by themselves at a time in their lives when they should be filled with hopes and dreams about their own futures. Again, my maternal instincts to protect and guard were in full operation as we all sat and talked and cried together for a couple of hours. Melissa, Christopher, and Carmen expressed confusion regarding the promises the Lord had given me regarding my healing. How convicting that I was now required to act on everything I had taught others!

In the Gospel of Matthew, Jesus spoke of the trials and persecutions that come on account of the Word that, when planted, begins to work deep in us. Often, I reminded the kids that we run with our understanding of what the Holy Spirit is speaking and get ahead of God's timing for us. I implored them to go before the Father themselves for a deeper understanding of His heart for His people. In our immaturity, we filter God's Word through our own understanding at the time of our hearing of it. Being conformed into His image and likeness by "putting on the mind of Christ" is a process worked in our character and nature—a grace-filled process that produces fruit through the dealings of the Lord in our lives.

I asked each of them to remember that our walk with God is all about the process. Faithfully, we must withstand those fiery trials by coming through like gold for His glory.

So many thoughts were running through my mind as I spoke to my children. Though needing to share and weep with them, I had to reach deep within to find the strength to give them a reason to hope. I also knew that I was again, in a much deeper way, going to experience that moment of feeling utterly forsaken by the Father, no matter how much I believed in His faithfulness. *Oh Father, I believe; help me in my unbelief.* This would surely be a cry heard by the Lord many times from deep within my heart. Despite the times when my circumstances looked overwhelmingly hopeless, I had to dig deep, coming face to face with Him, to tap into and draw from the well of truth.

Each day when I awoke, I opened my eyes and was reminded of the horror that had enveloped my life. *Oh please, Lord! I want to go back to sleep. I do not want to face this day; I am scared of what is to come!* My heart would race in my chest from the anxiety building inside of me. Carmen would cheerfully come into my room to help me get ready for my day. Upon seeing the beauty of hope in her countenance, her eyes pleading for the same hope within me, I would swallow hard to push down the terror and the tears.

Much needed to be accomplished over the next few days as I needed to see a surgeon to schedule the implantation of my mediport. My brother-in-law, Jim, an electrical engineer for the Mercy Hospital system at the time, helped to secure a first morning appointment with the surgeon. Due to the seriousness of my condition, the office nurse put me in a room right away, and the doctor compassionately showed me the port I would receive and explained the surgical procedure. I was scheduled for surgery the next morning, and before I knew it, I had a strange lump sticking out of my chest wall. This would mark my membership in a new society. I was now officially a citizen of "Chemoland." As I looked at my new "appendage" in the mirror—an unwanted invasion to my body—I fought feelings of now being undesirable to my husband. *What will he feel inside when he sees this? Surely, it will remind him that I am now defective.* It was painful to admit my thoughts to the Lord. Certainly, He above all would understand. *Lord, You willingly accepted the clothing of mockery while trusting the covering of the Father. Release me from this shameful cloak of vanity that I may do the same.*

Jerry got me up early the next morning for my biopsy. He helped me get ready as he packed his bags for the conference he had to attend in Chicago. My sister, Roseanne, a nurse, and my friend, Marilyn, were going to be with me at the hospital and every day after until Jerry returned. He gently held my face in his hands and let me know he was going to be with me every minute in prayer. I wanted Jerry to go, since it was obvious we were at the beginning of a long battle, and I had a lot of support around me. He would be rooming with his good friend, Fred, a devout Christian, and one thing I knew about my husband was that time in the presence of the Lord in prayer was vital to him. He always led our family by the proceeding Word of the Lord—his daily bread. Amidst all of the shock and commotion around us, there would be many serious decisions before us. Beginning this journey in the Secret Place allowed a covering where I could prepare to fight this battle by the Spirit and not by the flesh. Jerry and I wept in each other's arms as we said good-bye. Though he would be gone just four days, I dreaded any separation from him. However, deep in my spirit was the firm conviction in what I knew and believed: Nothing happening was without the knowledge and consent of my Father, and this was only the very beginning of a marvelous revealing of His awesome power and presence in our lives.

When we got to the hospital, the staff prepared me for my procedure, and I waited in a chair, blurred and in pain. It was an effort to speak. Compelled by my fear, I turned to my sister, Roseanne, and requested, "Please tell the doctor that if this is beyond hope, please just let me die." She promised to speak with him, and before I knew it, I was in the procedure room. As the anesthesia was being administered, Roseanne came into the room and whispered into my ear, "We can do this." I smiled as she kissed me and left the room. The power of life and death is in the tongue, and Roseanne's words breathed life into me at every critical juncture. I had no idea what her support would mean to me over the months ahead. She advocated for me in every area and, before we even had results, we left the hospital with a prescription for Thalidomide, an oral chemotherapy drug used specifically for multiple myeloma. I knew this was divine providence. Just the night before, I had cried out in pain, causing my son to panic and call Dr. Gonzalez for help. We wanted to get a drug started right away to help shrink the tumors that were affecting my ability to function.

Again that night, the pain in my sternum became unbearable, and each time it reared its ugly head, I doubled over in pain and tried not to vomit. It was getting harder to keep my composure during the attacks, and one night, as my friends were visiting, it overcame me like a steamroller. I unbuttoned my shirt in an attempt to get air and asked for help to the bathroom. Nita had become a pro at the bathroom routine; the need to hold my ribs with her hands to prevent fracturing while I vomited blood was not going to intimidate her. I felt like I wanted to die. Jerry was gone, and I was afraid of another attack in the night. The pain medication provided little to no relief. Attempting to numb a bit of the pain, Chris and Carmen packed my upper body in ice each night. Trying desperately to bring comfort, Carmen would constantly reposition me, arranging and rearranging pillows for support so that I could rest without undue pressure on my skeletal structure. It was a moment-by-moment challenge, and Carmen faced each struggle like a warrior. Wisely, she called upon the help of close friends so that she could meet with the doctor to discuss my care. In her absence, they blessed me with their words and gentle touch, lovingly massaging my feet to bring comfort.

At a mere nineteen years of age, Carmen, in poised fashion, learned about each chemotherapy drug I would be taking, learned how to give me injections to thin my blood, and asked questions of the doctor and his assistant regarding the possibility of hair loss. While this last concern may seem trivial on the surface, the loss of my hair represented a stripping of my womanly identity and a loss of my attractiveness in the eyes of my husband. Joined as one with my husband, I wanted Jerry to desire me, but the marks of cancer were shaking my confidence, despite his continual reassurance. Youthful but wise beyond her years, Carmen understood. I marveled at the character and strength she displayed under so much pressure. I watched her from what seemed like a tunnel, sinking deeply into a drug fog, while she moved about handling my care and coordinating my new life.

Carmen often surprised me by her intuition regarding my personality. When she was a young child, Carmen always observed me intently as I dressed and put on my makeup for special occasions. She was learning about more than obvious things. This intuition would come to bless me on a number of occasions.

My friend, Marilyn, arrived to relieve Carmen. She lovingly slipped right into the daily routine, making soup and massaging my feet to bring a welcome moment of relaxation. Like a sister to me, she ran my household with a quiet confidence, all the while respecting my particular housekeeping ways and concerns. The mother of a child with cerebral palsy, Marilyn knew just how to help me out of bed for bathroom runs and bathing. Never have I felt so vulnerable and transparent than at this time. Each moment brought a different wave and degree of fear, concern, or physical challenge. The medications added to the unpredictability of those moments, and I needed to feel safe in those times.

Not normally a dog person, Marilyn developed a "relationship" with my two furry children quite rapidly, and they were not forgotten in the daily routine. Hearing the sounds of life from the kitchen that day provided energy in my home, which kept me hanging on hour after hour. Marilyn had been very busy downstairs when she came into my bedroom to check on me. One look in my eyes told her the whole story. "Laura, you have taken too much Oxycontin. We have to revisit this issue with Roseanne and the doctor."

"But, I'm in pain," I retorted.

Marilyn knew I was a novice in this arena, as I never took anything for physical discomfort. My high tolerance for pain was what kept me pushing through as the cancer was wreaking havoc in my body for so many months. I had, during that time, continued to attend church and serve communion, despite feeling as though I was going to break in half. Marilyn watched over me continuously, and when she could not be at the house, she phoned to check on my condition twice each day. I often worried about her as she gave of her time and energy so selflessly. Her own daughter required so much of her attention day after day, and I did not want her to become exhausted early on. Yet, she pressed forward in love, serving the needs of each member of my family.

By the afternoon, my sister, Roseanne, was sitting at my bedside, quietly going over my pain medication schedule. With her help, I learned how to rotate Vicodin and Oxycontin so the dosages and intervals would be more effective at eliminating my pain. She asked questions often to evaluate my comfort and give me a sense of control over my daily routine. By the end of her visit, we had a schedule written in bold marker with room to make any adjustments necessary as my condition changed. This effort made my care easier on all those involved, since everything had to be brought to me on a tray. Roseanne's intuitiveness amazed me. She could approach me at any time, quickly grab a pillow, and tuck it in just the right place to relieve pressure from my joints and bones. Some nurses are blessed with true gifting, especially this nurse—my sister.

The nights were unbearable as I always felt worse physically, and my ability to cope was lessened by the pain. The condition of my skeletal system was very fragile, and it was important to make sure I remained still and protected from Jerry accidentally bumping me in his sleep. Tears streamed down my face as I fought the effects of the painkillers. Most disturbing were the bad dreams that began to haunt me. Wanting to provide a sense of security and comfort, Carmen, then engaged, asked her fiancée to stay with us at the house until Jerry returned from his conference. I prayed I would not have to ask Carmen or Christopher for help into the bathroom in the middle of the night. Knowing that they, too, desperately needed rest, I wanted them to sleep well. Sometimes I would grab the walker at night and slowly proceed forward, leaning against the walls so as not to disturb them. When they realized I had gotten up by myself, I would silence their protests by reminding them that I was still their mother, and I needed to follow my instincts to care for them!

Early each morning, our dear friend, Michele, came and prepared my breakfast, shopped for groceries, and remained "on call"
for anything we needed. Due to the recent layoffs in the auto-
motive industry, she was available just at the right time. I often
marveled at how the Lord strategically placed people—the hands
and feet of the Lord—in our home to meet our needs. An engineer by trade, Michele was extremely organized and possessed a
very giving heart. Her energy was boundless and her kindness
never-ending. Michele often sat by my bed to read Scripture or
just listen to me process what I believed the Lord was speaking
to me.

Marilyn would arrive Friday to help me, and she agreed to
stay until Jerry returned home from his conference that evening.
Sinking into yet another drug fog, I could feel my personality
changing with each passing day, but Carmen's tender loving care
kept me grounded. She helped me shower before Marilyn arrived,
and she patiently styled my hair and applied soothing cream to
my body. Before long, Marilyn walked through the door with
her usual energetic flair. She brought dinner for everyone and
promptly prepared my breakfast. Marilyn refused to react to the
circumstances and continuously spoke the promises she knew the
Lord made to me three years earlier—promises of restoration and
a sure and certain call on my life. We had spoken so often together
about our faith and the Lord's direction in our lives. With great
conviction, Marilyn continually reminded me of the plan of God
and His purposes in this circumstance.

As the evening approached, Marilyn surprised me with a pair
of pretty pajamas and helped me to primp my hair and apply some
lipstick (something that Jerry always loved to see me wear). I felt
like a stranger inside of myself as she propped me up in my chair
with pillows and left me sitting comfortably when Jerry walked

through the door. Though happy he was home, I could not seem to understand why I was hesitant to be alone with him. How did he feel as he walked up the stairs to our room? He had things to share with me, and yet it was as though we were both naked and vulnerable before each other. Marilyn's upbeat spirit was now gone, and the quiet was deafening. Even our dog, Hunter, a loyal and happy greeter, lay in the foyer after Marilyn closed the door and would not come up the stairs to see Jerry for the rest of the evening. He sensed a loss of joy in her absence.

Jerry's homecoming from his four-day work conference was a frightening reminder of the fact that, no matter how much support we had around us, our trusted friends and family could only go so far down that dark, lonely road with us. It was now imperative that, if we wanted to have victory in this battle, we must see and believe in the spiritual realm as vividly as we did in the natural. Faith is calling upon those things that are not as though they are. I could no longer just read the Scriptures and say that I believed. My circumstances called for action—real faith accompanied by works that would breathe life into my spirit, soul, and body.

I could hardly speak, and when I did, I cried out with regret for all of the mistakes made over the past seven months. Remembering that day when I hurt my back months prior, I struggled with the knowledge that the only physician who recommended an MRI was Dr. Gonzalez. Should I have pushed the local doctors for more answers and more immediate testing? I had to repent for operating in fear and not wanting to uncover or face the giant that was taking over my body and my life. The Lord softly spoke to me and said, "Laura, you must know your enemy in order to defeat him." Tears of regret fell as I threw myself at the feet of my Savior, the very seat of mercy.

Proverbs 15:4 says, *"A gentle tongue [with its healing power] is a tree of life..."* One of the fundamental keys to my restoration was surrounding myself with friends, family, and spiritual leaders who spoke words of life, hope, affirmation, and healing to me. The second key in this process was actually *receiving* and *believing* those powerful words of life as seed that would eventually produce a rich harvest of restoration for me as I regularly fed them with the truth of God's Word. Only He is the ultimate healer of our brokenness; only He can make us whole despite the messages of our past. As I remember this season of my journey, an unfortunate reality comes to mind: Personal history of rejection, betrayal, and verbal abuse affect so many people today. If you have endured a similar experience in your life, I'd encourage you to ask yourself a few questions as you pursue healing with the Lord:

1. How am I measuring my sense of worth? From whom do I seek approval and why?

2. When guilt and shame consume me, to whom do I turn? Do I reach out to those who will wisely point me to God's Word?

3. What promises has the Lord affirmed for my life? How do my daily choices reflect my belief in His promises?

I know that as you seek the Holy Spirit's guidance for answers to those questions, His healing presence will mend your brokenness and affirm you as Father's precious child who is deeply loved and cherished.

Chapter 3

I Choose Life

Yes, though I walk through the...valley of the shadow
of death, I will fear or dread no evil, for You are
with me; Your rod [to protect] and Your staff [to
guide], they comfort me. You prepare a table before
me in the presence of my enemies. You anoint my head
with oil; my [brimming] cup runs over. Surely...
only goodness, mercy, and unfailing love shall follow
me all the days of my life, and through the length
of my days the house of the Lord [and His presence]
shall be my dwelling place (Psalm 23:4-6).

My support system rallied around me with great strength as my family came daily to help in any way they could. I looked forward to my weekly visits with my mom and dad. Mom had just been diagnosed with Parkinson's disease, and it was so difficult to see her deal with the tremors while trying to cope with the news of my illness. I will never forget the way they sat by my bedside, faithfully bringing words of encouragement. This particular day, they read to me the *Litany for the Sick*. Like a psalm, each request reflected the depths of our despair, and the more my mom read, the more broken we all became. By the end of the litany, we cried, heads together, yielded to the Father, yet begging for His mercy. I will forever cherish the times of prayer and devotion with my parents. Their strength and support brought healing and restoration to my spirit.

Two of my sisters were on their way from Arizona and Florida, and I could not wait to see them! I looked forward to every weekend as my home was filled with family, visiting, cooking, and baking. What life this brought to Jerry and the kids! What a balm of refreshment for my soul!

My first day of chemotherapy ushered in a parade of support from my sisters, Roseanne and Terry, and Carmen. The doctor's staff called it my "entourage" of support. When the chemotherapy was administered, a circle of prayer physically surrounded my chair, washing over me. I was humbled by the tender care given to me. Having been raised in a large family where all eight daughters were athletes, my sisters and I share a fighting spirit, and their ongoing cheers of support encouraged me. Love never gives up! I am reminded of the call to the army of the Lord in battle when they were told, "Do not break rank."

When my sisters were around, there was energy in the environment. They all worked together cleaning, cooking, and joking with me about all of my peculiar housekeeping requirements. One night, they helped me into my living room and propped me up in a chair. I was beginning to sleep as it did not take much to tire me, but nevertheless I enjoyed hearing them at my stove preparing dinner for Jerry and the kids. They operated like a well-oiled machine, and my house never looked so organized or ran so smoothly. Sisters just know things! They even came bearing gifts—Terry with a cross to hang on my I.V. pole, on which the word "hope" was inscribed, and Elvie with a devotional and other gifts to enjoy. I hung on to the promise that each one would return in time, and I looked forward to seeing them again. Often, I asked them to promise they would take care of Christopher and Carmen if something happened to me. They continually reassured me of their devotion to the kids, but reminded me that I would make it through this trial and encouraged me to never give up.

Each evening I dreaded going to sleep as I was beginning to have night terrors. In these horrific dreams, a dark and menacing man followed me. I could hear his footsteps, and I sensed his desire to destroy me. Visiting with Pastor Dave one day, I explained these night terrors, and he inquired if I knew the man's identity. I told him that I thought he was the enemy. Dave asked, "Do you know his name?" I looked at him from my bed with a puzzled glance. "Myeloma," he continued, "and you can tell him to go and never return." Thereafter, Dave prayed for me, and before quietly leaving the room, he reminded me that he would walk with me every step of the way. "You're not alone, Laura. We are all with you every minute of every day."

A visit later that day from my nephew, David, and his wife, Annie, brought more insight into my intimidating night visitor. David, a cancer survivor himself, had recently undergone treatment for Hepatitis C contracted from the blood transfusions he received many years ago. David had beaten the odds and won a battle with Burkitt's lymphoma as a small child. His eyes were full of unspoken compassion and, never wavering, he reminded me of the need to fight without any concern of medical statistics that would discourage me to do otherwise. Sharing his childhood battle, he recounted seeing an old woman looming in the corner of his room during his treatment, and we both agreed it was an intimidating presence. Smiling, we decided to name my evil visitor Miles E. Loma, and as counseled, I spoke to him every night, ordering him to go and leave me in peace! Hour after hour, family members came to visit. It became apparent that they wanted to see me in case things did not work out as we all hoped. Many concerned family members—cousins, nephews and nieces, and my uncle—came from all over the country. Everyone was there to wish me well and offer loving support and prayers for a successful outcome.

I had visitors on a daily basis and was always surrounded by family and friends on treatment days. There was never a lack of volunteers. Wednesdays became my special days as my pastor's wife, Bonnie, always came faithfully. She spoke the promises of the Word of God into my spirit and reminded me each week as we took communion together that "by His stripes I *am* healed!" When I could not reason, due to the medications, she spoke the Word into my spirit, and if I began to fret, Bonnie again spoke the Word. Through the fog of all of the pain medications and chemotherapy, she looked into my eyes with a boldness and confidence from the Lord that penetrated into my spirit. There was no barrier to the Word because Jesus *is* the Word! Bonnie carried the presence of the Lord in her and breathed life into my body, soul, and spirit with every visit. She would remind me that "faith comes by hearing and hearing by the Word of God" (Rom. 10:17 NKJV). Patiently, she listened as I attempted to recall the frustrating details of my condition and all of the medical opinions that came with every appointment. Her very presence comforted me.

With Mother's Day approaching, I grieved, night after night, recounting so many precious memories with my children. Will I live to see them marry? Will I see the ordination of my son, Christopher? Father, give me the strength to enjoy the kids so they do not lose hope. For the occasion, Jerry planned a special movie, and Carmen made my favorite organic homemade ice cream. They all gathered around my bed to enjoy the evening, and I drank in every minute of my time with them. Jerry presented me with a beautiful cross to wear around my neck and said, "I asked the Lord what I should give you, and He told me to bless you with this cross, that it may remind you of the road we are called to walk with Him and the victory He promised you. When you are scared, just pray and hang on to the cross." After that night, I never had another dream about Miles E. Loma. What power there is in the presence of the Lord—power to pierce the darkness that threatens to overtake us.

Like me, you must know your enemy. You must clearly identify your fears in order to overcome them. In doing so, you can then be transparent with those you trust and with the Lord in prayer. It is through this transparency that the Lord can guide you into victory.

While struggling to hold fast to the Lord's promises, I often felt overcome by the battering waves. It seemed I had barely come up for a breath, adjusting to the I.V. chemotherapy, which I had only been on for two weeks, when another haunting reality came at me. Jerry was already downstairs in our office counseling a client when the phone rang. He had left it by my bed in case I needed to call anyone, as the kids were both running errands. A strange voice spoke saying, "Mrs. Kymla, I am a spinal surgeon out of Providence Hospital. I have been given a copy of your MRI by your orthopedic surgeon, and I would like to see you and discuss the tumor you have at C7. It could pose a danger to you as it grows by impinging on your spinal cord. You will need surgery and radiation to that area, and we will need to repair the fractured vertebrae by doing a kyphoplasty at T12. You also have another fracture at T7, but it appears to be healing on its own."

I responded with horror and shock, "I don't even know you, and I cannot respond to this information right now!"

By now, Jerry was coming upstairs to check on me. My screams of despair met Jerry's reassurance. "It will be okay, I promise," he said as he tried not to panic, but I could see the concern and despair in his eyes.

"Don't say it will be okay," I cried. "It is not okay!" The wailing gushed forth like crashing waves in a storm, "Please, God, no more. I can't take any more!"

We made an appointment with the spinal surgeon. Thankfully, my friend Julie drove me to the appointment, and Jerry met me there after work. What a comfort Julie was, making sure I had everything I needed. We visited, walking up and down the hallway together, since I could not sit too long in the waiting room chair. It seemed like forever before I was given an examining room. A resident entered and asked me to join him in a separate room to view my MRI.

"No, thank you," I answered. "I am aware of the report and will let my husband review everything."

Though I realized the wisdom in being informed, I knew that I trusted my husband to discuss with me any pertinent information. As my covering, he knew I was exhausted and needed his help interpreting the report. With my oncologist's guidance, we decided to give the chemotherapy a chance to attack the tumor on the neck before undergoing a risky surgery, which would delay the continuation of my chemotherapy schedule at a critical time. However, the damage to the thoracic spine required immediate attention, so a kyphoplasty was scheduled for the following week. We all agreed that this procedure would lessen my pain and discomfort by stabilizing the fracture. The surgery would take place during a scheduled break from my chemotherapy, so I would have time to recuperate. Any week without chemotherapy was cherished time for me, for I could stay home and feel a sense of normalcy again. If my counts were good, I would be good to go, and we could proceed as planned.

My friends volunteered to drive me to the hospital so that Jerry could meet me there after work. Given the possibility of a stem cell transplant sometime down the road, Jerry did not want to request too many days off of work early on in our journey. As a result, he relied on the assistance of others, working as much as possible to avoid problems with his employer. My oncologist was encouraging us to do enough chemotherapy to bring the plasma cell count down to an acceptable rate and then have a transplant. We were overwhelmed enough by the induction stage of treatment, but we definitely wanted to prepare for what might be around the corner. There was much research to be done, and several opinions were needed before we would be able to make a decision regarding a transplant.

It is amazing how God gives us the grace to walk through crises and deal with the everyday realities of life. Without His intervention, we certainly would not have been able to deal with the pressures of Jerry working two jobs and my illness. We know that, while walking through the circumstances of life, the Word of God proclaims that we are seated in heavenly places with Him (see Eph. 2:6). We had no strength left of our own, but His was sufficient for the day. *Lord, help me to focus on just one hour at a time. Let Your sweet voice reign in my heart so I can follow Your lead.*

After I was released from the recovery room following the kyphoplasty, my devoted friends drove me home and helped me into bed. Feeling more discomfort than I expected, I wept as Marilyn quieted my tears with warm blankets and prayer. Rubbing my aching legs with her tender hands, Marilyn remained with me while I eventually drifted off to sleep after taking something for pain. I felt like a small child in need of rescue from circumstances too great for me to bear. When I could not pray, I would fall onto the wings of the prayers of the saints. *Intercede for me in my weakness, you holy men and women of God!*

Though quite sore for the next few weeks, I was immediately able to walk with more confidence. Jerry took me by the hand each night and helped me walk down the street until I would tire. "You need to gain some strength," he insisted, despite the fact that I could not walk a straight line without his assistance. I was humbled by the memories of jogging down that very same road, time and time again. I could no longer even walk it alone—in more ways than one. How quickly my muscular body was deteriorating, and how profoundly I was reminded that my life existed solely because the Father breathed His breath into me. Even though I knew He was with me every step, I also knew that, in His sovereignty, He could not prevent me from having to experience this dark and uncertain place.

I lay awake each night, fighting the desire to give up on what appeared to be a hopeless battle. Lord, if I go through all of this, and I can't be cured by the drugs, how far will You make me go, and how much destruction will my body experience from all of the side effects? I was in so much torturous bone pain that it took every ounce of resolve and concentration to push through it so that it would not overcome me. Breaking through the stillness of the night with boldness, the Lord's voice came to me very clearly: "Laura, you have to decide if you want to live or die. Will you choose life or death?"

Staring into the darkness for what seemed like an eternity, I replied, "I choose life, Lord."

"Then fight," He said.

Surely, He was teaching me to fight in a way that was foreign to my natural mind. One baby-step in the natural had to be taken, while following His lead to take giant leaps in the spirit. This was going to prove to be a challenge, as I could no longer read or concentrate well. Each time visitors came, I asked them to read to me from my Bible. I waited with eager anticipation each week for the messages Pastor Loren brought to the congregation that came by mail on CD. Many times, I would review them over and over so the Word would penetrate every fiber of my being. Deuteronomy 8:3 says, "...*Man does not live by bread only, but man lives by every word that proceeds out of the mouth of the Lord.*" That passage became more real to me than ever. If I did not hang onto the edge of His garment, I would perish. The fresh revelation brought by my Shepherd was nourishment and life to me. With each hurdle I had to jump, Pastor Loren sought the Lord for encouragement and hope. Juggling all of the medical information and seeking the Lord for wisdom in each choice, Jerry and I felt like we were walking a tight rope. Loren and Bonnie kept reminding us that there could be no wrong decision when our hearts were seeking His will.

During one meeting with my pastor, I shared something that spoke to me while watching a movie about the birth of Jesus that past winter. The writers poignantly displayed Mary's humanity and the reality of the faith required to walk out the call on her life. What struck me was the prophetic Word brought to her throughout her exodus from Nazareth to Bethlehem. How she must have wondered so many times if she heard the angel correctly when he told her she was to carry the Savior of the world! As we are told in the Scriptures that follow, Mary pondered many things in her heart as she raised her son and tried to grasp the truth of Him being fully God and fully man. I shared with Loren how there was not an area of my skeletal system from the pelvis up that was not affected by the cancer.

I then asked my pastor if he would pray for me, as I needed strength for the journey. He immediately rose to his feet and prayed. Pastor Loren reminded me that the Lord did not want me to look at people who had received a cancer diagnosis and died from their illness. "You are not to compare your circumstance with those who were not healed here on earth, Laura."

How wonderful the gift the Father bestowed upon us when He gave us the Holy Spirit, who leads us and guides us in all truth! Like a warm shield around me, His living Word illuminated the path and brought His peace as I walked in the Spirit through the fiery darts of this rough time. I became aware that, though the enemy desired to destroy me, he had no authority to take my life or do anything without the consent of the Father. I uttered so many times in my spirit, "I trust You, Lord; I do trust You." Ever merciful and just, He plans out every element of our paths, ever pointing us to our destination. I knew, ultimately, that He was my destination, but did I really understand what that meant? Did I understand what it meant to be conformed to His image and likeness? Did I understand that I am here to advance His Kingdom, and I am not here to build a kingdom unto myself?

It is important that we allow our personal experiences to bring us into a place of greater compassion toward others in their own pain. When we find a way to turn our focus to the Father, without becoming *consumed* by the circumstances, the Lord will use what looked hopeless to be a testimony of hope for others.

Two months after the kyphoplasty, while I was on active chemotherapy, my family continued to bless me with their prayers, encouraging visits, and loving service. A surprise visit from my nephew, Matthew, came next. Flying all the way from Arizona, he had one goal in mind: service to us. He came with great enthusiasm and cleaned my garage from top to bottom until late in the evening. How humbling to see my nieces and nephews care so deeply to make a trip to Michigan. I lay there and watched as Matt came into my room periodically and provided enthusiastic updates on the newly organized space. What an awesome demonstration of Christ's love! Memories flooded my heart as I looked at him, reminding me of when he was a little boy and how we talked often together about the Lord. How poignant was the reality of our effect on one another as we see the fruit manifested in different seasons of our lives.

What a blessing the youth in my family are to the older generations! As I continue to battle the side effects of the cancer and treatment, my spirit is bolstered by regular visits from Ann's three teenaged daughters. Jenna, Julia, and Maria bring such life and joy to my home! Their laughter and youthful giddiness make me chuckle right along with them, even in some of my darkest moments. Lovingly, each one reaches out to me in her own unique way. I can always count on their encouraging words and acts of service, from household chores to gentle massages. It is precious to listen to them share their passion for sports and music. Most poignant, however, are the conversations we share about our passion for the Lord and all that He is doing in our lives. Because of our bond of trust, Ann encourages me to speak into the lives of her children, and I am blessed to do so for my precious nieces. Our love for one another is beyond telling, and it transcends each moment that we are together.

Treasured moments with family continued, and Father's Day was upon us. I again began to dwell on my life with Jerry and the load he had carried throughout the years to keep all of the pieces together regarding my enzyme therapy. The medical bills were beyond our natural ability to afford, but Jerry consistently worked two and sometimes three jobs to pay them. I grieved the fact that he had lost so much time sacrificing his life for my benefit, but he always reassured me that he would have it no other way. On Father's Day, Christopher made dinner for his papa, and they helped me into the kitchen to join them. The toxicity levels from the chemotherapy were causing great difficulty and hindering my energy levels. During dinner, I was unable to lift my head higher than a few inches above the table top. Christopher held my hand and caressed it, continuously asking, "Are you alright, Mama?" I was only able to whisper to all of them that I did not know. I can only recall feeling as though I was slipping away from this earth, and it required too much effort to fight. I sat quietly while Jerry read the cards the kids wrote to him. As I read Carmen's note to her papa a few days later, her feelings of vulnerability and her need for security were revealed. She wrote, "I am so blessed to have a father who is always there for me whenever I need you. I know that you will always hold our family together no matter what."

My heart sank as I read the words that expressed her heart, her fears. I wanted to reassure her that everything would be all right, and at the same time, I wanted to cry out for her and beg the Lord to spare her from experiencing my death. Sometimes it felt like I was in a pressure cooker, trying desperately to handle the depth of this experience and all that it brought to each one of us. The emotional side of the battle was overwhelming enough, and every week brought new medical information and challenges. *How can we possibly handle all of this, Lord? My husband, my children—their lives are deeply changed because of my illness. I need them, Lord, but I also want them to live their lives with joy. Only through you, Lord, can we find joy in this struggle.*

The month of July brought the return of my sister, Terry, and my niece, Andrea, along with Andrea's husband, Jason, and their three children. Andrea cooked delicious meals, and I enjoyed the presence of her children in my home. It made life appear normal to hear all of the laughter and play. Terry, along with my sister, Ann, continued moving through the house like a white tornado, and the two of them were near when I received a call from my oncologist after my second bone marrow biopsy. I had been on treatment for two months, and it was time to check on the efficacy of my drug protocol.

"Are you sitting down," Doc asked.

"Yes," I replied anxiously.

He continued, "I just wanted to give you your results so you could celebrate with your family for now. When we did your first biopsy, your plasma cell rate was 74 percent. At this time, your plasma cell rate is 5 percent. Congratulations, Laura."

I wept, crying out in relief, and thanked him for calling. Hearing my cries, Terry and Ann came rushing into my bedroom. Eventually, the whole family was standing around my bed, waiting anxiously for the report. Once my voice was able to project through my tears, the words gushed forth with a torrent of emotion. My family responded with an outpouring of praise and thanks to God, along with much embracing and many tears of joy. We filled the room with a grand chorus of gratitude! This was the best news we had heard in three months.

My oncologist made appointments for Jerry and me to visit Harper Hospital and speak with the head of the Bone Marrow Department regarding a stem cell and possible donor transplant. The consultation did not go well, as the doctor was very direct and negative. He wanted me to be admitted for a transplant within six weeks and told me I would die without one. Jerry and I have always taken the time to learn about the latest advances in medicine for multiple myeloma, so the opportunity to ask questions was critical in that moment. We needed to be sure there was no stone unturned regarding the risks involved. Our niece Andrea, a nurse, who had flown to Michigan from California to help care for me, was present during that appointment. The three of us concluded that we were not at peace in any way, shape, or form after that visit and that we needed to continue consulting with other physicians and hospitals.

Our next trip for a consultation would be to Buffalo, New York, to meet with one of the foremost myeloma specialists in the country. He proved to be a refreshingly unique man, and much to our amazement, he was a Christian who shared with us his love for the Lord. He noticed the cross I wore around my neck and said, "I see you wear the sign of our great Healer."

I shared about my love for the Lord, Jesus Christ, and the promise He made to heal me. The specialist looked over my reports and MRI results and told me that I was a living testament of a miracle, especially considering the critical nature of my earlier biopsy results. The most recent biopsy results after three months on chemotherapy were astounding, with my plasma cell rate dropping from 74 percent to 5 percent.

"You are wise to question the efficacy of a transplant, Laura," he stated, while humbly sitting on the footrest of the examining table as we looked down upon him from our chairs. "It is rare to see a myeloma patient rally from where you were. The new chemotherapy drugs, if used throughout treatment, are effective in managing this disease. The life expectancy is the same, and there is no need to take a sledgehammer to the problem. Medicine is changing its thinking with multiple myeloma. You must remember that, medically speaking, myeloma never goes away. It grows back like hair, and other than periods of rest, you will always live on chemotherapy. Your prognosis will depend on how you do this year."

At the end of our visit, I asked the specialist if we could pray for him. He responded graciously, "I would love that." We all held hands and prayed for healing, wisdom, and favor upon his practice. We all hugged and left each other, amazed by the Lord's faithfulness yet again. He confirmed that I was not to have a bone marrow transplant, and he extended my circle of Christian medical support, adding another link of strength and hope. This was a divine appointment. I was certain that my results would remain favorable over time, since I responded so well to my therapy. Surely, I would astound everyone and would never need treatment again!

I asked for a break from chemotherapy from the end of October through the holidays. It had been over five months since I came out of remission, and my body needed time to adjust, even to the respite, as it had gone through so many changes from the steroids and other drugs. A short time later, I remember standing in my kitchen one day and sharing with Bonnie that I was not able to turn my neck well enough to pull out of the driveway. I was constantly in a state of discomfort in my neck and spine, but I pushed any serious concern aside until I had more tests in January, the first of which was a bone marrow MRI.

Since standing for any length of time was difficult to say the least, this particular MRI presented a real challenge, as it was a new type of imaging done very slowly for a three-hour period under anesthesia. I had to keep my body very still so the test would not have to be repeated. In addition to the MRI, I was admitted to the hospital and scheduled for a bone marrow biopsy the next morning. Results were sent to the myeloma specialist for review, but since he was out of the country, we had to wait quite awhile for the report.

In the meantime, Jerry and I purposefully planned to celebrate Christopher's college graduation at the end of January since I hoped to be on break from chemotherapy and wanted to enjoy the time with family and friends. In every decision and every family activity, we had to take into account my treatment schedule and my potential physical condition. At times, I felt like a ball and chain—a burden to my family. Would they grow tired of caring for me? *Lord, I have become like a dependent child! You know the heart of a mother, Lord. How I long to care for them again!*

The next day my friend, Marilyn, and I planned a special overnight shopping and dinner to celebrate the holidays together. We were so looking forward to having uninterrupted time to talk as our bond was great. I was worried about being able to enjoy our shopping trip and prayed that the Lord would supply stamina and remove the pain from my neck and back. Finding a proverb that touched my spirit, I laid my Bible on my chest near my neck and believed God for my answer. As I got up to put my shoes on, I heard a popping sound and felt some relief.

The faithfulness of the Lord covered our entire evening, and I shopped for three hours without pain! Marilyn and I went back to the hotel and got ready for dinner. We talked for hours all evening, sharing our hearts, before finally drifting off to sleep. I had a difficult time getting comfortable in the bed at the hotel, so when Marilyn dropped me off at home the next day, I planned to rest for a while. She had no sooner pulled out of the driveway when I received a call from my oncologist.

"Laura, we have the results of your MRI, and we have a problem. You have a tumor at C7 that is impinging upon your spinal cord. This tumor has grown despite your success on chemotherapy. You are in danger, and I am admitting you to the hospital immediately. We are going to start a Decadron I.V. right away, and you will need neurosurgery and radiation."

Despite the news, the peace of the Lord poured over me, and I gathered my thoughts and made a plan for what had to be done.

First, I called Jerry. Immediately, he left the office and headed for home. I took a deep breath and sent an update via e-mail to all of our friends, and then I called my sister, Ann, who came over right away to help me pack my suitcase. Christopher and Carmen were home from church within minutes after receiving the news. Before leaving, the staff lovingly prayed with them, sending both of them home with the presence and peace of the Lord. In the meantime, Roseanne called from the hospital and told me not to leave until she had made all of the arrangements and my room was ready. As always, she moved on my behalf to make every step as stress-free as possible. This gave me time to prepare in many ways.

It was not long before Jerry came in the door visibly shaken. As we prepared to leave the house, he began to cry. Jerry tried so hard to be a calming force in the storm, but even he could not always hide his emotions by escaping into the medical details and alternatives. While I did my best to overcome the physical challenges, each passing day brought a deeper realization of my incapacity. So many things that he loved about me—my energy, mental sharpness, and zest for life—were often buried in the rubble. Despite this harsh reality, I depended on my husband's constant faithfulness. I needed him to be one with me in unshakeable belief! *We will hold fast to the Lord's promises; like a phoenix, we will rise from the ashes!*

Our dear friends, Becky and Nita, came over to pray with me, and they began to declare direction, wisdom, and victory over our situation. As Becky boldly proclaimed that no one would touch my case who was not meant to do so, my heart was pierced. Though we had just received the news that the tumor on my cervical spine was in fact growing and putting me at risk, we also knew that the radiologist had seen the tumor in the MRI a couple weeks prior. Doc had hoped it was smaller after receiving the chemotherapy, but Jerry and I were prepared, just in case, to seek other opinions from neurosurgeons who specialized in removing tumors from difficult locations on the spine. We were praying that if the tumor did in fact need to be removed, a new technique called pinpoint radiation could be applied to reduce the risk of removal. Now that we knew we had little time to seek other opinions, our hope was that I could be transported to the cancer center in Detroit. We did our part to prepare for visits to two major cancer hospitals in our state, but God had other plans.

As the time came for Jerry and me to head for the hospital, he and the kids made a plan to prepare my organic meals so that I could stay on my diet throughout the hospital stay. Loyal and dependable as always, my family ensured that all of the details were handled. We had learned to cover one another in love so my stay could be as peaceful as possible. I fought back the tears while saying good-bye to everyone. Turning back when I reached the porch, I tapped on the glass of our front doors for one last good-bye to my dogs, Hunter and Delaney. Hoping beyond all hope, I whispered quietly, "I will be back."

The ride to the hospital was painstaking as Jerry began to grieve uncontrollably. Unable to see well through the tears, he missed a turn on our route. It grieved my heart to see him this way, but I knew that he, too, needed moments of grieving. Jerry had always been a tower of strength and a controlled thinker, but the Lord was clearly leading him down a different path. This path stretched beyond his ability to think or reason—far beyond—engaging his heart at the deepest level. There was nothing he could do to save me or control the suffering I was about to experience. I remained quiet the whole ride except to let him know I loved him and that I would return.

Once we arrived, it was not long before I was kindly escorted to my room, refusing the use of a wheelchair. I was placed on the new oncology wing of the hospital, and I swallowed hard as I approached my room. With each step toward the door, I came closer to the realization that I was no longer in control. Upon entering the room, I could not believe my eyes! Nita and Becky were there ahead of me, praying and asking for the presence of the Lord to fill the room before I arrived. I could not believe the sweetness in their spirits and the sacrifice they made for my comfort. How humbling is the love of the Lord as He rushes over us gently in our nakedness! Naked and bare was I before Him at that moment.

I quietly sat in a chair, intimidated by the bed that represented weakness and frailty. *Please, Lord, I do not want to lie down in that bed!* I was always so active and strong, but yet there I was, facing surgery for the second time in nine months. I yearned to turn around and go back home to the safety of my own surroundings. Taking a few deep breaths, I waited for the nurse to come in and welcome me to my temporary home-away-from-home. I prayed that I would adjust to my surroundings one step at a time, and slowly, I surrendered my clothes and put on my pajamas. The doctor had given orders to start an I.V. of Decadron, so the nurses wanted me resting comfortably, which would help the medication do its job of reducing inflammation around the sight of the tumor and spinal cord. Proceeding carefully, the doctor did all he could to reduce the risk of creating any danger to my life while decisions were made regarding treatment.

Interestingly, prior to my admission to the hospital, we had made an appointment with a top neurosurgeon in the Detroit area, but the neurosurgeon at the local hospital where I had been admitted provided timely information that facilitated our discernment regarding the best surgeon for me. Clearly, the Lord closed one door and opened another, and my case landed in the capable hands of a well-respected surgeon. He explained that the tumor presented a risk of cancer spreading to the brain and that it was applying pressure to my spinal cord, placing my vital functions in danger. With this assessment, surgical removal was necessary, followed by radiation to the area. He asked us to think about our decision and call his office by close of business that evening if I wanted him to operate the next afternoon.

Jerry and I called on our close friends, pastors, and family members to pray for wisdom and direction. After praying all day, the decision was made to go ahead and schedule surgery the next afternoon. The doctor's assistant came to my room for me to sign paperwork, and with the strength of the Lord, I resolutely read all of the risks of the procedure, knowing that He had ordered my steps. His faithfulness would bring success and nothing else! I was reminded that I may not wake up from surgery; I may find myself on a respirator in ICU or on an orthopedic surgical ward for more careful monitoring. I did not accept any of these options, and Jerry and I prayed and believed for the best possible outcome. Pastor Loren, though ministering in Peru at the time, called Bonnie to let me know that all our brothers and sisters in Peru and El Salvador were praying. What a comfort that the body of believers was lifting up my situation before the Father! Becky's earlier declaration—a bold proclamation before the Father that no one would touch my case that was not directed by Him—came to pass in a very real way.

Jerry stayed with me until it was bedtime, and I had special visitors that night. Even my parents and my sister Jane came to see me the night before the operation. The neurosurgeon came back to my room to make sure I did not have any other questions and to reassure me that he would take good care of me during surgery. His friendly and approachable personality put everyone at ease, and I was happy my parents were able to meet him. The seriousness of the operation was painful for them to endure. I could feel the concern and despair they were carrying inside as they looked at me in such a vulnerable position. How I wish I could have protected them from having to face this with me, and yet, I truly needed their comfort and reassurance. This realization that I had become a caregiver to my parents, even in my weakened state, was a bittersweet milestone. I reached out to them, still needing the love and acceptance that only a mother and father can provide.

Carmen spent the night at the hospital with me so that Jerry could go home to prepare my organic food and take care of things at the house. It was such a comfort to have her with me, but I did not sleep the entire night as lab technicians, nurses, and doctors came into the room repeatedly for testing before the surgery. I prayed earnestly all night and listened to the most recent message from my pastor. The timeliness of the word that was brought forth encouraged me, and I wanted it to go deep into my spirit as I prepared for the race set before me. Praying earnestly in the Spirit, I cried out for mercy in my grief, and His peace fell over me. I pressed in to declare the promises that were given to me and believed that I would return to my room and recover with strength.

Many visitors came the next day and surrounded my bed with love, reminding me of His faithfulness. Joseph, one of the ministers from the church, and his wife, Elaine, came and prayed, anointing me with oil. Joe reminded me that our circumstances are all in God's hands, but it is very often a painful process in order for Him to complete what He has foreordained. I wept as I worried about losing my hair in the event of more chemotherapy. The journey brought a continual stripping of my physical appearance. I felt embarrassed by my new body, and now the thought of being bald was so frightening, so humiliating.

Elaine prophesied that I would come through with flying colors and encouraged me to rest, as it was all in God's hands. I was anointed with oil four times that morning, and my own

Pastor Jeanne came to pray and stand with me for healing. I received each one with thanksgiving and gratitude, realizing with some humor that I must be a pretty sick lady to deserve so much attention! As the morning progressed, a steady stream of friends came and encircled my bed to support me and pray. I was overwhelmed by the sacrifice they made to be at my side. By the afternoon, I grew tired from not having eaten and was more than ready for surgery.

Soon, the pre-op team came in and let me know it was time for me to go. As each person hugged me, I hung on for strength and life. I chose to walk to the gurney and then turned to say good-bye to Christopher and Carmen. It was as if a dam burst as the three of us hung on to each other. I wailed as I looked at each of them intently. Composing myself, I let them know I would be back in my room and would see them shortly. As they began to wheel me out of the room, I could see the parade of friends and family lining the hallway. Weeping for my children, I heard in my spirit, "Woman, behold your son. Son, behold your Mother." It was all beyond my control now. I looked back and observed my dear friends embracing both of my children. I could not comfort the kids; I could not do my job, but they were being loved with all of the power within Bonnie, Becky, and the entire group.

As I write this, I must stop and heave tears. The memory is so bittersweet, and yet, what comfort I felt with such an outpouring. *"...All the days ordained for me were written in Your book before one of them came to be. How precious to me are Your thoughts, God! How vast is the sum of them!"* (Ps. 139:16-17 NIV).

My neurosurgeon came into the pre-op room and smiled as he let me know he would take good care of me. He joked a bit to make me laugh, and then I asked him if I could pray for him.

"Sure," he responded.

I shared with him that the Lord, during His crucifixion, declared, "Behold, I make all things new." I blessed his hands as I took them in mine, and before I knew it, I was dozing off to sleep. The team then suspended me in the air, face down, and carefully lowered me onto the operating table on a cushion, protecting the tumors on my rib cage that protruded permanently under my breasts.

After many hours, I awoke in recovery and saw my sister Roseanne's familiar face as she carefully washed all of the blood out of my hair. I rejoiced as I was wheeled back into my original room! The surgery was over, and I was in stable condition. My neurosurgeon shared the news with Jerry and the entire room of supporters. The tumor was removed in one piece, but the spinous process at C7, which serves to attach muscles and ligaments to the vertebrae, was completely destroyed by the cancer and fell off in his hand during surgery. He had to cut half of the spinous process above and below that point, so it would be a challenge for me to regain good support in my neck.

After the surgery, my sister Ann came and stayed overnight with Carmen and me. It was a comfort to have her there as she gently helped me to the bathroom and tended to my care. With Ann watching over me through the night, Carmen was able to sleep soundly despite all of the blood pressure checks and lab tests. She was one exhausted trooper! Christopher and Jerry returned home, where Christopher prepared meals for me so I could remain on my diet. Each one did his or her part to ensure I received the best possible care. With determination, I worked hard to unplug my I.V. monitor and hobble around without assistance. There was a drive within me to regain my independence as soon as possible so I could go home. After all, Jerry and I had worked hard to create a home that is an extension of ourselves—a place of faith, love, acceptance, and peaceful security. How I longed to return!

The morning after my surgery, Ann left the room to attend Mass in the hospital chapel with my sister Roseanne. Before leaving, they asked if they could invite the hospital chaplain, a Catholic priest, to visit and pray with me. I replied, "That would be nice." Though I was no longer a practicing Catholic, I was happy to receive the prayers of one of God's ordained ministers. The priest, a humble and vibrant man from Uganda, arrived later that day and pulled a chair up to my bedside. Smiling at me, he asked, "Were you baptized a Catholic?"

I answered, "Yes, I was baptized and confirmed."

With conviction, he responded, "Then you are still a Catholic. Shall we pray together?" As he began to pray and anoint me with oil, I glanced across the room at my sister. Bent over with her head in her hands, Ann sat in a chair weeping uncontrollably. This sister of mine, who would always hide her tears in the privacy of her own room, was now at the mercy of the Spirit, and her tears streamed forth like a waterfall. Clearly, Ann needed to witness this anointing as much as I needed to receive each and every blessing given at the hands of God's faithful. The bond of our upbringing is still a sweet connection for us, and we often sing together the hymns of old. Though we differ in our practices of faith, many core beliefs are still the same. Together, we cling to the mercy of our Lord and Savior, Jesus Christ.

I did not take pain medication except Motrin, and by Friday afternoon, my oncologist asked me if I was ready to go home the next day. Surprised by my own hesitation, I replied, "Tomorrow would be good, but Jerry needs to have a plan for our big dogs first."

Doc knew I did not want to risk falling since my neck was far from healed. As much as I hated being in the hospital, I was apprehensive about taking that first step out the door. That familiar yet new level of fear was foreboding as I prepared to walk through unchartered territory once again.

Later that day, another dear friend stayed with me at the hospital while Jerry had some much-needed time of fellowship with our spiritual son, Lindsey. While my friend and I were talking, the volcano of feelings within me erupted, and I began to wail and grieve with her in a way I had never done before. Suddenly, I became aware that I was seriously ill. It was as if a veil was lifted, and I was in the middle of an ocean overcome by the waves of panic drowning me. "Please don't let me die," I yelled. "Please don't make me go through any more!" I could not control the guttural screams gushing forth out of the innermost part of me. I tried to cover my mouth with a pillow, but the grief had a purpose of its own. Subconsciously, it was as if I knew I must let go of the overwhelming emotion only after Jerry left the room. My friend held onto me, as I could not contain the depths of my grief. In her eyes I could see she was searching the heavens for guidance as I groped in the same way for an anchor. *Oh Lord, You are the stronghold of my life!*

Before long, the tempest had left. I became still, my soul quieted by the healing balm of the Holy Spirit. Jerry and Lindsey returned, and we visited until I was ready to sleep. The next morning, Carmen helped me shower, and we even fixed my hair and makeup. How I missed being able to pamper myself—to stand back, look in the mirror, and be satisfied with the womanly reflection staring back at me. *Will I ever see myself in the same way once again, or is God preparing me to look with new eyes?* I went back to bed dressed and ready for the doctor to discharge me. Before I knew it, my oncologist was outside my door.

Moments later he came in, sat on my bed, and took my hand saying, "Look at you, all made up and ready to go home!" In a more serious tone, Doc continued, "Laura, your plasma cell rate has doubled, and we have to start chemotherapy after radiation. We will begin a new I.V. protocol, but I want to check with other hospitals to make sure I am choosing the correct protocol for your situation. I would also like to consult Dr. Chanan-Khan in Buffalo after he reviews your MRI."

I swallowed hard in surrender as I tried to put this information in a compartment to be dealt with later. I just needed the courage to go home again and fight.

Often, a negative report is accompanied by feelings of fear, intimidation, and despair. If we're not careful, our thoughts begin to race out of control, and we end up creating devastating negative images from a seed of fear. Though the thoughts exist only in the mind, ruminating on them can have devastating results on our emotional (and physical) health. In Second Corinthians 10:4-5, Paul declares:

> *For the weapons of our warfare are not physical [weapons of flesh and blood], but they are mighty before God for the overthrow and destruction of strongholds, [inasmuch as we] refute arguments and theories and reasonings and every proud and lofty thing that sets itself up against the [true] knowledge of God; and we lead every thought and purpose*

away captive into the obedience of Christ (the Messiah, the Anointed One)…

The strength of those words implores us to take an offensive strike on any thought that is contrary to the character and Word of the Lord. When you face seemingly insurmountable obstacles, seek the Holy Spirit's guidance as you honestly ask yourself the following questions:

1. Of what am I most afraid? Have I clearly expressed this fear with those who are closest to me?

2. Have I given this fear to the Lord and asked for the peace and the confidence that comes through believing His promises for my life?

3. Has my own physical or emotional pain caused me to become so introspective that I lose my focus on the Lord and what He has spoken over my life?

4. How am I able to allow my situation to minister to others, even in a place of personal weakness?

As you pursue His presence, choose life in Christ today. There is no circumstance or situation, no trial or difficulty, and no sickness or disease that is outside God's ability or willingness to heal, restore, and overcome.

Chapter 4

BEAUTY IS IN THE EYES OF THE BEHOLDER

And He humbled you and allowed you to hunger and
fed you with manna, which you did not know nor did
your fathers know, that He might make you recognize
and personally know that man does not live by bread
only, but man lives by every word that proceeds out
of the mouth of the Lord (Deuteronomy 8:3).

"WILL I LOSE MY HAIR?"

"Yes," Doc replied, "but hair will grow back. You are still the same Laura inside; never forget that." I knew that we would need to find a wig, but I began to pray immediately for favor and mercy.

The ride home from the spinal surgery was bittersweet. One of my sisters was at the house baking my favorite oatmeal muffins, so I felt relieved that she would help me acclimate while Jerry was in the office downstairs counseling. Carmen's close friend, Jennifer, was also there to see me and offer Carmen support. The walker provided for me was placed inside the door so I could use it as a shield from my dogs as I entered the house. Walking in slowly, I was taken aback by the sensitivity of my dog, Hunter, who stepped away from me, knowing it was not safe for the usual greeting after an absence. Halfway down the hall, I had to step into the closet as the tears broke through when I saw Jennifer's face. *Lord, give me strength so I can walk this road with Your grace for the kids.*

I gathered myself and made it the rest of the way to the kitchen, where my sister, Jane, came and sat with me at the table, graciously serving muffins and tea. Before she could ask how I was feeling, I began to weep. "I'm scared about this next phase of treatment, and I am so disappointed in the biopsy results."

Now, my sister is very much a logical thinker, and her gift in this area brought comfort just at the right time. "Laura, let's remember the test results when you first came out of remission. The plasma cell percentage was at 74 percent last May. You are now at 9 percent, so there is a lot of life in you, and you can fight this battle. We are not giving up on you." Her words provided calming encouragement, and I went to my room to rest while she remained at the house, baking for the rest of the day.

No matter how my emotions surfaced at times, there was always that place of rest in the Secret Place with the Father. As each day passed, a greater dependence on Him was created within me. For every physical movement, every ounce of wisdom, strength, and peace, and even for the hope within, I had to rely on His grace to sustain me. The next couple of weeks would be busy with appointments while I continued healing from surgery. Now was the time to press on and forget all that lay behind so I could be ready for the next phase of my treatment.

Over the next week, we had several meetings with my oncologist and phone consultations with Dr. Gonzalez. Since we knew that the tumor in my neck did not respond to the chemotherapy, the pathology report indicated that, although the tumor was consistent with myeloma, it had obviously taken on a life of its own and cloned into a stronger cell type. This is not uncommon for myeloma as studies indicate that, while it responds initially to chemotherapy, it eventually creates a resistance to the chemicals. My plasma cell rate, though still considerably low, had doubled in three months, showing quick relapse and steady multiplication of the cancer. Though the option for a stem cell transplant was discussed and considered in interviews at two cancer hospitals, the second opinion we received in Buffalo confirmed our belief that the new trend toward chemotherapy treatment of myeloma was just as effective as far as overall survival rate and much less caustic to the immune system. For now, we would continue our attempt to achieve an effective response and "back the cancer off" as long as possible.

As we continued to take all of my treatment options before the Lord, the oncologist "reminded" me that I would never defeat cancer on a "prayer."

I replied, "I must follow the leading of the Holy Spirit inside me, Doc." I would do more chemotherapy for now and increase my enzyme therapy in an aggressive attempt to keep my immune system very strong. These steps were needed to fight the cancer and prevent frequent hospital stays due to infections, which typically plague cancer patients.

Doc continued to caution, "The new program will be very hard to tolerate, Laura. If you cannot handle the discomfort, let me know and we will back off."

"I will do it," I responded. "Just tell me what to do to make myself more comfortable." So far, we knew we had to keep my body strong for the battle.

One well-documented fact that we uncovered through research, which was often not shared with us, was the likelihood of myeloma's resistance to chemotherapy over time. Yet, because we had been informed that myeloma "grows back like hair," I was told that I should expect to live on chemotherapy. These opposing realities kept us on our faces in prayer and reinforced what the Lord spoke to us years before: "In the day the doctors say they've done all they can, you will see My mighty hand of healing and salvation."

During our weekly visits, my pastor's wife, Bonnie, often reminded me to take one day at a time. In Matthew 6:34, Jesus instructs, *"Do not worry or be anxious about tomorrow..."* This is how we rest, knowing that every tomorrow is in God's hands. One of my journal entries at the time reads:

> The hope burning within me gets brighter every day, not dimmer! Jerry and I pray all day and night, but our hearts are not just praying for this circumstance! There is so much work to be done for the Kingdom of God! We pray for Pastor Loren, as God is so strategically sending him to the nations during a very tumultuous time in history. The cries of the people ring in our spirits, and we ache to deliver them. There is much to do and no time to waste! I remind the Lord that I do not doubt His promise. "I cannot do my work from the grave!" Jesus replied, "Behold, I make all things new!" It is ringing in my spirit every day. It is a new day in God! We must hear the Holy Spirit speak so we can

follow His voice and not the voice of the enemy who comes to rob, kill, and destroy! Fear, doubt, and unbelief are not from God! He gives life! Thank you all for speaking life to me and loving all of us as you have so faithfully. "Christ in you, the hope of glory."

While awake one night at 3:30 A.M., I began to hear the Holy Spirit speak to me about the living and active Word. Did I really understand the meaning of this truth? Again, the Holy Spirit reminded me that the power of life and death is in the tongue. He quickened to me that the Lord died to give us not only salvation from hell after death, but resurrection life and dominion over our circumstances, so we can overcome in all things and do the works He prepared for us. Surely, He was completing a purifying work in me, which called me into the Secret Place with Him so I would be prepared to be an outpouring to the Body of Christ. Like Jesus, we are called to lay down our will and seek His way for the glory of His name and the purposes of the Kingdom of God.

Carmen and I would go to a nearby cancer center for my radiation treatments, so we scheduled an appointment for radiation mapping of the area surrounding my cervical spine. I had never experienced radiation before, and I was a bit nervous about the side effects and treatment. My journal entry that day was short:

> The radiation mapping was a long process. There were several interviews with the nurse, doctor, and tech, followed by the positioning. Sounds simple, right? Well, not so with a very "thorough" doctor and a patient with tumors front and back. The question: How do you get someone positioned for treatment on the neck, when she cannot lie on her back, and her rib cage

and sternum have calcified tumors? Well, the Lord is good! A big, thick piece of foam, a super headrest, and support under the ankles provided the answer! The extra cushioning worked, but my face looked like a beet when I was finished!

I was not prepared for the exhaustion and the tears that overflowed as the two men looked over my spine and my surgical scar, discussing the fractures—the battle scars—while I vulnerably lay face down on a table. I began to praise the Lord amidst the tears. *Lord, I am not sure why I am feeling emotional, but I can't help it!* The tears streamed down my cheeks as I prayed with every ounce of strength for them to stop. I was tired of being treated like an empty shell, a scientific study. Crying out for help, I turned to my Shepherd. *Lord, You must have felt humiliated when beaten and scarred, hearing the comments and jeers of those around You. Totally exposed, You bore our sicknesses and our grief. Oh Lord, be with me as the doctors discuss my wounds and condition as though I were not present. The back of my body is totally exposed, naked and vulnerable. My once athletic body is now twenty-two pounds heavier from the steroids, and I am weak. My rib cage is deformed, and there are scars on my back. My once "perfect" posture is now rounded by brittle bones, and I have lost inches in height. Please help me to praise You, Father! You are worthy, and You are my exceeding and great reward!*

When the mapping was finally finished, Carmen drove her tired mama home, and Jerry, bless his heart, listened compassionately on the phone as I wept. He prayed, talked, and then called the doctor from work to make some decisions regarding different types of radiation, additional testing, and the like. I left everything at this point up to the wisdom of Jerry and the doctor. That evening, Jerry and I would attend church together for the first time in months. It was to be a culmination service of thirty days of prayer, and we had been active participants from home. Little did I know until one hour before service began that Pastor Loren was led to anoint me with oil and pray for me.

We walked into the church, and I chose the same row, the same chair that I had sat in for years. It was an ethereal experience. I felt a dichotomy within myself as I realized so much of me was dead yet so alive in Christ! This truly is what Paul meant when he spoke of the pull between wanting to be with the Lord and yet knowing he had a purpose to fulfill. I watched as my fellow ministers and elders anointed the congregation with oil, and I pondered the years of growing in my faith at Mt. Zion, through the love and mentoring I have received. The Lord spoke to me out of Ezekiel 16, where the heart of the Father toward Jerusalem is so beautifully articulated (though they did not trust in Him). It is expressed as follows:

> *And when I passed by you and saw you rolling about in your blood, I said to you in your blood, Live!...I caused you [Israel] to multiply as the bud which grows in the field, and you increased and became tall and you came to full maidenhood....Now I passed by you again and looked upon you; behold, you were maturing and at the time for love, and I spread my skirt over you and covered your nakedness. Yes, I plighted my troth to you and entered into a covenant with you, says the Lord, and you became Mine. Then, I washed you with water; yes, I thoroughly washed away your...blood from you and I anointed you with oil. I clothed you also with embroidered cloth and shod you with...leather; and I girded you about with fine linen and covered you with silk.*

I was keenly aware that evening that the Lord had deposited a seed within me and that He was molding me in body, soul, and spirit for His pleasure. My love for inspirational true stories of triumph and victory never ceased to move me to tears from deep within my spirit. *Lord, use me; I want to deliver people!* Often pondering the Book of Ruth, I came to understand that the Father's faithfulness was made evident in Ruth's relationship with Boaz, her kinsman redeemer. God even proved faithful to her mother-in-law, Naomi, who was embittered from all of the losses she had incurred as a result of choosing her own way. In the story of The Good Samaritan, found in the New Testament, the Samaritan man was not regarded as one of God's chosen people and, in fact, was shunned publicly. However, not only did he bind the wounds of the injured man, who had been left helpless on the roadside by all who passed, but the kind Samaritan also found him a place to live and *returned* again to bring complete restoration, setting him on a new path (see Luke 10:30-35). This pattern is a type and shadow of the heart of the Father for us, His people! He is our Kinsman Redeemer as He picks us up in our dysfunction and pain, covers us with His love, rebuilds us according to His plan, and restores us! Truly, He is the Potter, and we are the clay—the work of His hands.

The Father must always be true to His character. He is *for* us, no matter what we see with our natural eyes! This truth helped me to settle something in my spirit that night as I watched my son minister to the congregation through his music. In that moment, I saw a young man, my very own son, from a totally different perspective. As a family, our roots have grown deep at our local church, and my children have flourished in the House. No matter what, the Lord's plan is sure for my children, and He is able to take care of them and provide for them in ways I never could. Within the Body of Christ, we lack nothing! All of our needs are taken care of because His Spirit and love are alive in His people! How thankful I was at that moment!

During the service, Pastor Loren called us forward and began to pray. He reminded the people that I was *winning* a battle against cancer. He prophesied that rivers of living water would pour forth from my bosom. The presence of the Lord was so strong as I stood in awe of Him. Pastor then called all who were battling cancer forward for prayer. In their fear, they came forward, and Jerry and I prayed over them. Deep in my heart, I knew I was a deliverer, and it was time for me to impart what God had been pouring into me. I did not want to be a victim of this disease! My favorite Scripture rang in my spirit all night:

> *...For I know...Him Whom I have believed,...and I am [positively] persuaded that He is able to guard and keep that which has been entrusted to me and which I have committed [to Him] until that day* (2 Timothy 1:12).

As soon as I got home, I crawled into bed. It had been a long and emotional day. The Lord was not done blessing me, however. *Cinderella* was on the television! Humor aside, all who know me understand that it is my favorite story of all time! Though Jerry graciously offered to watch it with me, as he had done on one of my birthdays years before, I insisted he watch a "man action" movie with Carmen instead. Of course, no arm-twisting was necessary! He, too, needed a treat after being my rock all day. Though I was exhausted and emotionally drained, it was a very good day.

Over the next few months, I spent time healing while watching others carefully and tenderly provide for my personal needs. I was now busy going to radiation to ensure that no stray cells were allowed to spread. The affected area of my neck was precariously close to the brain stem, and we did not want the serious risk of any more spinal cord involvement. My family and friends took turns driving me to the cancer center, and sometimes Roseanne and I would make special plans to shop for items I needed at the store. My mobility was poor, which caused me to tire rapidly. So lunch and rest were always on the agenda. The visits were quick and the staff very organized, and I quickly became used to my new routine. One month of radiation treatments was preceded by my new chemotherapy protocol of Doxell, Thalidomide, and Decadron. My agenda also included testing to determine a baseline for the assessment of any resulting heart muscle damage.

So many thoughts ran through my mind as I pondered the seriousness of the possible side effects of chemotherapy. It had been almost a year since I came out of remission, and I had to take every thought captive and put total trust in the Lord, as all of these things were out of my control. *One day, one moment at a time. If I focus on how powerful You are, Oh Father, nothing can make me afraid because all things are under Your feet.*

Setting my fears aside and wanting desperately to rebuild my physical strength, I began using the treadmill at home. Unfortunately, due to the loss of core support in my cervical area, the muscles in my neck tightened severely during exercise. As a result, my neurosurgeon agreed to prescribe physical therapy, and in late winter of 2007, I had the pleasure of meeting Ed Fahey, a physical therapist, for my very first treatment. Leading up to this visit, I was nervous and discouraged by my level of physical discomfort. However, the peaceful environment I encountered upon entering the therapy room was a refreshing experience. As classical worship music played in the background, Ed began to use his hands to engage my body's own energy to heal, opening up the lymphatic system and unblocking stress points in my muscles and tissues. I quickly felt tears coming to my eyes, and I worked hard to choke them back. Ed, sensing my pain, began to recite Scripture as the music played. The presence of the Lord was evident in this very humble man—the newest member of my "healing" team. *How faithful is the Lord to bring yet another avenue for my restoration!*

I left relaxed and hopeful that my therapy would help me cope with the consequences of repeated damage to my skeletal system. Two visits per week were scheduled with the goal of loosening the muscles and building strength in my body. This was another confirmation of the Lord's plan to bring healing through His Body, each one playing a significant role in helping me heal—body, soul, and spirit. The role Ed played in my caregiving was significant because he helped my body adjust through many failures and disappointments and gently spoke life into my spirit. As I walked down this dark path one step at a time, he was another beacon of light called to gird me with strength for the journey.

Ed has a treatment table near a window that overlooks a canal. To this day, I enjoy looking out at the trees. Because the window is usually open, I am able to hear the rippling water and the ducks swimming playfully. Long ago, I heard a well-known evangelist describe an experience he had where he was taken up into the heavenly realm. While he shared many things about that beautiful experience, one thing stayed with me. Before he returned in the Spirit, the Lord spoke to him about His love for the people who did not know Him and His heart to see them healed and restored. As he promised to do the will of God to bring people to the Kingdom, the Lord told the angels accompanying the evangelist to take him back via a route that would allow him to see the mountains. "He loves the mountains," the Lord said. How precious this was to me that the Lord would express knowledge of such a minor detail in his life.

I was learning, more and more each day, that the Lord cares about the details of my life, as well, even the finest of details. One day, as I arrived for my physical therapy appointment, the staff was preparing the tables for the arriving patients. "Sandy, set Laura up at the table in front of the window; she loves to look out the window," Ed said. I had not thought of the evangelist's experience in a while, but I knew that Ed was speaking to me from the love of the Lord within him. I praised the Lord, as I felt so honored that such a small detail would be considered important in my care. I will never forget this moment as it was very healing to my spirit.

Sometimes the details of our everyday lives are a part of the Lord's beautiful weaving. Without each thread—each simple moment—the beauty of the complete masterpiece would be lost. If we can somehow see His hand at work in little moments of wonder—a quick burst of laughter, meaningful conversation, an encounter with someone in need, nature revealed in all its splendor—then we can better understand the intimate way through which God reveals His character in love.

I began to carry a burden for Ed's practice and prayed as the Lord began to show me His blessing on Ed. Ed had experienced

several heart attacks in the past and was in need of another therapist to help with his bustling practice. Mary, another physical
therapist at Ed's office, worked only a few days per week in the
afternoons, which was not enough for the demand. I shared with
Ed what the Lord was showing me, and he said it was a confirmation of his own thoughts and prayers. Together, we discussed
the Lord's leading with regard to Ed's health and the legacy that
he is called to provide—a legacy of treating the whole person in
an environment where the Spirit of the Lord is evident. All of
the patients are treated with the highest regard and dignity. Ed
speaks to others with humility and respect, regardless of age or
mental capacity.

I had experienced physical therapy on three other occasions
during the last fourteen years at three different locations. However, I never completed my cycle of treatment because help was
only provided in the specific location prescribed, and any referred
pain was ignored. Exercises and techniques used were often irri-
tating to the area being treated. On the contrary, my treatment
at Ed's office was wonderful. The staff's effective, gentle therapy
was such a blessing.

As I continued to pray for relief for Ed, the Lord reminded
me of a word I received years ago, which was that I carried a "big
stick in the Kingdom of God" and was exhorted to "go ahead and
pray and see what the Lord would do when I prayed." I take the
liberty to remind our Father of that word every time I pray for
others. As I seek the help of others in my need, the Lord gives me
a burden for them. As they work to help my body function more
efficiently, I silently pray for them.

In June, I completed my round of Doxell and Thalidomide. I
had been on this regimen for over two months and was weary of
the side effects from the Doxell. The Thalidomide had already

created issues of its own. One day in particular, I knew something was wrong when I could not seem to control my heart rate, so I left a message for my sister, Roseanne, and asked her to return my call. Her "nurse's intuition" won out, and she came over right away. When she arrived, she came quickly to my bedside. Knowing that the medication made it difficult for me to tolerate loud noises or confusion, she spoke with me in her usual quiet way. After checking my blood pressure and heart rate, she could easily see that my heart was racing. I had reached a level of intolerance for Thalidomide, and I can honestly say that, at that moment, I didn't care. I was scheduled for a biopsy the next week, and we could address the issue with the oncologist when we received the biopsy results.

At this juncture, I felt led to meet with my pastor. I always waited until the Holy Spirit spoke to me to do so, as I did not want to use my meetings with him for complaining. I wanted to go in when the Lord was prompting me to do so because He had a word for me. I made an appointment, and after we talked a bit, Pastor Loren prayed. He began to prophesy to me that I had let the Lord shine His light over every part of my heart, and that I would never be the same from this experience. He reminded me in prayer that "rivers of living water would flow from me for the people." Loren then sat down and said, "Laura, I feel so strongly in my spirit that you are ready to give birth to something." In my own thinking, I hoped for victory and healing with my biopsy report. I wanted to believe that what I was about to birth would be a direct result of my healing at the present time. Given my own mindset and desires, I felt ready for the bone marrow biopsy.

That evening I received a call from our friends, Becky and Calvin. Calvin had been in prayer for me and felt that he was to come and anoint me with oil. Jerry, Calvin, and Becky all gathered around me to pray and, again, the word of the Lord came forth. Calvin had asked the Lord why I had not been healed, and he asked Him whom he was going to send. The Lord answered, "You...I am sending you."

Becky then brought a word about strength and spoke about going up the mountain and receiving refreshment from the brook when we needed it. "People will say, 'How are they making it? How do they continue to persevere through this crisis and still praise the Lord?'" I knew that the brook symbolized the presence of the Lord and that it was going to be essential that Jerry and I draw strength from the Lord in our times of prayer, as well as abiding with Him in the Word.

Continuing in prayer and encouragement, Becky shared that from this day forward things would never be the same. Again, I thought this would mean I made it into remission. How important it is to "walk softly before the Lord" and discern His ways. "His ways are not our ways, and His thoughts are not our thoughts," the Word of God tells us (see Isa. 55:8-9). *But, surely I have suffered enough, Lord!*

When I walked into the procedure room for my biopsy, I was confident that all would be well and that we would see good results from my round of treatment. Surely, the 9 percent plasma cell rate would have decreased by now with all of the chemo and radiation. My confidence level was so high that I planned on going by myself to the doctor's office for my port flush the following week. When that day arrived, Carmen saw me preparing to leave the house on my own. In her usual strong-willed manner, she stopped me and declared, "I'm going with you today!" I tried to convince her that I was fine going by myself since the port flush would take only ten minutes. She would not accept my decision.

As we sat and waited for the nurse, my oncologist walked by the chemo room and noticed us there. He walked to the desk, grabbed my chart, and handed it to me. "Read this," he demanded.

Carmen and I read quickly through all of the pages of results, looking for the total protein percentage. Surely, Doc was handing me my results in front of everyone so I could celebrate my good report. When I saw the results, my heart sank. It read 17 percent. This was almost double the rate I started with in January. I could not believe that, after almost twelve weeks of chemotherapy, I had gone in the opposite direction.

When I showed the nurse the results, her face furrowed with concern as she questioned me in disbelief. "He gave you these here?" Grabbing the results from my hand, she left the room. A few moments later, I was asked to join the doctor in an examining room.

Not usually emotional during my meetings, I was not prepared for the events that occurred that day. Doc was stern during our discussion and began to press me to have a bone marrow transplant since my body was resisting the therapy. Tears streamed down my face as he asked me firmly, "Are you willing to keep fighting?"

I could barely speak, let alone answer a question about which I had no time to pray. Trying to keep my composure, I asked Carmen to wait outside. Ever the warrior, she again refused. Without any sensitivity, Doc continued to drill me, demonstrating no respect for my uneasiness about having my daughter view another moment of crisis in this battle. I was in shock, and I could not believe what was transpiring before my eyes. The nurse sat very close to me, lending support as I tried to maintain some level of composure. The office staff attempted to reach Jerry to no avail. *Oh Lord, not another disappointment! I cannot wait to get out of here! I need Jerry's wisdom and his arms!*

For Carmen's sake, I gathered enough composure to hug everyone good-bye and went straight home to talk to my husband. Carmen, with much wisdom, went the opposite way of home when we had almost arrived. "Where are you going?" I asked nervously, as I wanted to get to my bed to cry and pray.

"We are going to the church, Mom," she stated confidently.

"Why?" I asked.

Carmen knew me more than I knew myself at that moment. She had observed my life for years, and one thing she knew for sure was that my life was centered around the Lord and the Body of Christ. Being part of our church family brought life and healing for us throughout all of her childhood. They, indeed, became our family through many lonely years of separation from our natural family. I acquiesced, graciously knowing that my submission to her decision was as much for her sake as it would be for mine.

One of the ministers was waiting for me when we walked into the church. With great compassion, he pulled a chair close to mine and quietly began to listen to my grief. Joe encouraged me in the Word and stressed the faithfulness of the Lord, reminding me that all that was important was to trust the Lord in this process. "Everything else is just details," he stated. Joe anointed me with oil and prayed for peace, strength, and healing. Though more at peace when I left, I needed time to process what had happened at the doctor's office. It took me some time to realize I was angry with my oncologist for the way he handled us that day. As I prayed and cried out to the Father, I realized that Doc was as disappointed in the results as I was. He had become emotionally involved in my case, and he was not able to achieve positive test results from the protocol he had chosen for me.

Consequently, it was decided that I should try a new drug called Revlimid, which had been approved for use on myeloma patients who were not responding to Thalidomide. I began taking the drug along with Dexamethasone, a steroid. After two weeks on the new chemotherapy protocol, I decided I needed a break. My heart was contending with the Lord, and I was not mentally ready to keep fighting this way. After much prayer and a phone consultation with Dr. Gonzalez, Jerry and I decided to take a week away to pray and reflect on healing and a course of action. Before leaving, I wrote a letter to my doctor and let my nurse read it. It read as follows:

Dear Doc,

Thank you so much for taking the time to call and speak with me regarding your conversation with the myeloma specialist on Friday afternoon. You have been such an awesome doctor, and you have supported my family and me throughout this whole ordeal. We are forever grateful for your expertise and direction.

Jerry and I have been praying much and listening with our faith for the still, small voice of the Lord to speak direction and peace into our spirits. No matter how great the support system, only we can go this road, being true to what we hear from our great and gracious Father. Our desire in all things is to honor and glorify Him with our lives.

I know He works all things together for good for His purposes, and I can see so much fruit (in the midst of the suffering) in the lives of my family and friends. I have been changed forever by this experience, and hopefully His life shines greater in me.

One of the cries of my heart is to have a restful and fun summer with my family. Though I have been able to do some things so far, it will be increasingly difficult to enjoy them as I do not function well on the meds, let alone the possibility of my counts dropping with each passing week. After I received my last protocol with Doxell, I went into my bone marrow aspiration feeling good physically. I want to function for a while feeling strong and clearheaded.

I would like to take a six-week break from my treatment in exchange for quality of life during the summer season. I will, of course, be in for my Zometa treatments and monthly labs for monitoring of my proteins. I feel I can make further decisions from a point of strength after that. August will be the three-month mark from my May biopsy, so I am requesting another biopsy at that time.

I will speak with you very soon. Jerry and I will be leaving for our getaway on the 24th and I am really looking forward to spending time with him and in prayer. Our spiritual life is the center of who we are as a couple, and it will be refreshing for us both.

We thank God for you, Doc, as you bless so many. We respect you beyond words, and I am better for having known you. I am looking forward to talking with you more.

Sincerely,

Laura Kymla

As a professional counselor, I often helped guide my clients to "take a step back" from the complex details of their circumstances and try to see a broader view of the situation as a whole from the Kingdom's perspective. The expression "he couldn't see the forest for the trees" certainly applies here. What's the point? In doing so, the immediacy and anxiety "in the moment" is relieved. Even more so, we are reminded that we have a Father who sees the end from the beginning and will never leave or forsake us. Psalm 30:10-12 illustrates this point:

> *Hear, O Lord, have mercy and be gracious to me! O Lord, be my helper! You have turned my mourning into dancing for me; You have put off my sackcloth and girded me with gladness, to the end that my tongue and my heart and everything glorious within me may sing praise to You and not be silent. O Lord my God, I will give thanks to You forever.*

As you reflect on your own life and apply the principles I've described, ask yourself the following questions:

1. Can I see the Lord creating something new in the midst of the upheaval in my life? Search out what the Lord is birthing in you so that you may find meaning in the trials you face.

2. Am I able to find my identity in Christ when everything around me is shaken?

3. When the outside world is no longer recognizable due to change or loss, am I grounded in my identity and in His unending love for me?

Chapter 5

A TIME OF PURGING: CLINGING TO THE ROCK

So everyone who hears these words of Mine and acts upon them [obeying them] will be like a sensible (prudent, practical, wise) *man who built his house upon the rock. And the rain fell and the floods came and the winds blew and beat against that house; yet it did not fall, because it had been founded on the rock* (Matthew 7:24-25).

OUR WEEK AWAY WAS SPENT IN GLEN ARBOR, ONE OF THE MOST beautiful areas in Northern Michigan. Jerry and I passed the time walking and resting by the water, staying in prayer. I wrote in my journal each day and will share two of my letters to the Lord:

June 25, 2007

Lord, Your faithfulness is a shield (a protection from all that comes against me). Your promises to me are sure because You are my refuge and dwelling place. Nothing is as sweet as abiding in Your presence.

The Spirit of the living God is within me working (with energy) to will and to do God's bidding. It has the power to heal and restore. Your Word says that no evil or plague shall befall me or come near me. I will trust in Your Word, Lord. You promise in Your Word that as I walk in obedience and abide in You, You will never forsake me (Ps. 34 and 103). When I call, not only will You answer, but You will deliver! You promise me long life (deliverance, healing, blessing) as a satisfaction (Ps. 91).

June 26, 2007

Lord, Psalm 103 states that You know my frame, and that You will satisfy my life with good things so I can soar in strength as the eagle. I have seen Your dealings, Lord, in my life. I have endured through suffering, and I grow in Your strength continuously. Heal me according to Your Word, Oh Lord!

Words are powerful, and they impact us at the very core of who we are. Loving words, touch, are vital to healing. The absence of those things, Lord, leaves its mark—body, soul, and spirit. But You, Oh Lord, send Your Word, Your love, and Your faithfulness to heal. I cannot be righteous enough on my own, but You have made me righteous through Your work inside my heart.

I cannot repeat words as a formula, but You are the Word, and in Your faithfulness to mold me, it has been written upon my heart. I love Your Word, Lord. It is my very breath. Your life in mine is Your active Word working in me by the power of the Holy Spirit. It is healing, it is life, it is hope, and it is the power that will quicken my mortal body.

Throughout our vacation, I spent each day dwelling on these thoughts while the Lord spoke His gentle love into my spirit. How glorious it was for us to be quiet before Him with no interruptions! This was precious time with my husband and with my Savior! Returning home refreshed, I spent the rest of the summer building my physical strength and focusing on healing. Jerry and I often went to the park to walk with our dogs Hunter and Delaney. As each week passed, my strength returned, and I could feel myself becoming more alert and more alive. What a blessing to break through the fog and see the light again!

Sadly, our hope for a restful summer was overshadowed by the disheartening spiritual fall of both of our daughters. Carmen, whose engagement ended after her fiancé experienced an unfortunate emotional setback, rebounded into another relationship that was abusive, and she would not hear my pleas to end it. Her eyes became darker with each passing month, and arguing could be heard from her room every night as she talked with her boyfriend on the phone. The saddest part was observing the many friends who encouraged the relationship, telling her that the abusive patterns were normal and a result of typical differences between men and women. As a counselor, I saw the warning signs of abuse and showed Carmen the list of characteristics of abusers, hoping to lure her away from this troubled young man. But she was not thinking clearly. After taking care of me and watching her fiancé experience tragedy in his own life, Carmen was not prepared to deal with all of the pain that was hidden within her. She was clearly in crisis. At the same time, Melissa was avoiding us and not living her life in order as a wife and mother of four children. Jerry and I were devastated, and as we prayed and received more information regarding the behaviors and decisions of both girls, Jerry began to meet with them individually.

In a very painful decision, we separated our daughters. We knew each one needed to take responsibility for her life and work at becoming whole. Carmen, after breaking off her relationship, once again became the bright-eyed, happy young woman we always knew her to be. The most healing component for both girls was the dedication of the Body of Christ to mentor and lead them to a deeper place in God. My sisters in Christ and fellow deacons immediately stepped in to counsel and meet regularly with Carmen. She had more mothering during the many months of her quest for healing than she ever knew possible! One of my friends also met with Carmen privately and taught her many things about her relationship with the Lord and her spiritual walk. Eventually, Carmen joined a powerful class at church called *Healing for Women*. Over the course of ten weeks, Carmen was assisted in identifying her grief and loss and was built up spiritually to continue on her road to healing. What a glorious change in her! Carmen found new friendships with young adults who were serious about their walk with the Lord, and out of those relationships, a Bible study group was formed. The group prayed passionately in the Spirit for hours several times each week. Carmen began to speak with such a conviction regarding her faith and, month after month, she grew in peace and joy. Her dedication to the Lord's Word and to prayer brought forth a gift of exhortation and prophecy. She boldly spoke life into those who needed it most.

Melissa spent countless days in counseling with pastors at the church and also received mentoring from Becky. Her countenance and spirit began to soften, and she was determined to restore her relationship with Jerry and me. In time, she and Carmen were able to renew their relationship in a much healthier manner. What a joy to see that what the enemy meant for harm, God turned around for good! He is faithful to perform His Word!

As September approached, my biopsy was performed and again, I received a call from my oncologist. "I hate to ruin your Labor Day weekend, but I have your report in front of me, and we are headed in the wrong direction." My plasma cell percentage was 30 percent in some areas of the bone marrow and 50 percent in others. Again, Doc tried to convince me to have a bone marrow transplant, but in our discussion, he said something that helped me hold fast to the direction I received from the Lord the summer before. "Though a transplant will not help you, it is my hope that the bombardment of chemicals and reintroduction of stem cells will buy you some time." I told him that there was no peace in that decision for me. I needed time to think and pray and would meet with him soon.

Typical of Jerry's coping style, he began to search for answers by researching on the Internet. While looking over some of his findings, I noticed a book advertised on a prophetic ministry newsletter we read, which was geared toward those with incurable disease. I showed it to Jerry, and without my knowledge, he wrote to the author, a medical doctor located in Florida. In his correspondence with the author, Jerry briefly mentioned my condition and asked if she would send any recommendations for healing from her book. Responding quickly, she shared that the Lord had asked her to pray for me and that I would hear from her the next day. Knowing that the author probably received countless requests from hurting and sick people, I was amazed that she cared enough and took the time to respond personally.

Faithfully, when I turned on my computer the next day, the doctor had written a word she received for me from the Lord and asked if I would be able to come to Florida to work with her. She wrote that she had not been able to get me off of her mind and heart because the Lord would not let her stop praying for me. The Lord spoke to her, saying, "This one is special."

I asked her specific questions regarding her treatment and fees. The doctor shared the gifting the Lord had placed within her to help those who were considered incurable by traditional medical standards. She also worked using the Word of the Lord and its principles to prepare people for surgery and postoperatively control pain with little or no medication. She explained, "My work consists of asking the Holy Spirit for direction in helping you identify memories that created broken places within your human spirit. Painful emotional experiences have a direct impact on the physical body when they result in this brokenness." She also shared that, at the Lord's direction, there would be no fee for her work with me. Extending herself even farther, the doctor graciously invited me to stay in the apartment attached to her home and suggested that I attend a healing class at her church.

Needing to make arrangements quickly, I contacted my sister, Terry, to ask if I could stay with her in Orlando and commute to the doctor's house. According to her calculations, the drive would take about one hour each way. Even though the doctor graciously offered her apartment to both of us for as many nights as we needed, we decided to commute so that we could stay at Terry's house. My sister was more than enthusiastic and began making immediate preparations for my arrival. After several calls to Carmen and me, Terry had done all of the grocery shopping so my medical diet could be followed with ease. If any one person could handle the challenge of shopping, making my meals, and getting me to my destination, it was Terry. She loves a challenge and never backs down!

Within twenty-four hours, Jerry, who was in prayer every day, knew I must go to Florida. He was certain the Lord had orchestrated this very unique and rare opportunity. Though I was in shock that we were even considering such a trip, there was a peace in the very depths of my soul. It seemed very apparent that the Lord intended for me to see His glory in His Body. Line upon line, He would direct my path into unknown places, making provision for each experience spiritually, physically, financially, and emotionally.

My pastor's wife always reminds me, "Laura, follow peace." Her words echo in my spirit every time I walk into unchartered territory, and I have learned that when we quiet our spirits, we can be sensitive to God's leading when least expected. Our willingness to surrender to His Lordship opens the door for His ultimate will to manifest in our lives. Paul echoes this principle in First Corinthians 13:11, stating:"…*now that I have become a man, I am done with childish ways and have put them aside.*" Putting aside the "childish ways" is part of walking in partnership with the Father as mature sons. In doing so, seemingly ordinary, everyday communication and unexpected connections unlock the supernatural opportunities He has available for us.

Clinging to this wisdom, I packed my suitcase. My sister, Rose-anne, and her husband, Jim, drove me to the airport, where Jerry had arranged for wheelchair assistance to the gate. Turning to say good-bye to Roseanne, emotion flooded over me, and I could see the worry in my sister's eyes. She did not like the idea of my fly-ing alone under the circumstances, but there was a determination within me to take this risk and see what the Lord had prepared for me. My focus of late had been on taking care of any unresolved pain and issues deep within myself, as I knew the danger of not dealing with toxic emotions from former wounds.

With my Bible in my arms, I boarded the plane and began to search the Scriptures for uplifting and peace. It was very unlike Jerry to send me anywhere by myself in my condition, and I was amazed at the stillness of my soul. I was excited to see my sister, Terry, and knew she was faithfully preparing to make my transi-tion smooth on her end. When I landed in Orlando, it was not more than minutes after I entered the baggage area that I could see Terry walking and then running to meet me. We were both so happy to see one another! We headed to her house to eat and then prepare for our trip to Ocala the next morning.

The ride to Ocala took more than one hour, but Terry and I talked all the way. Our focus was the Lord and what He was doing in each of our lives as we listened to uplifting messages and praise music. Terry, in her sensitive way, arranged every detail ahead of time. Together, we prepared to meet the doctor. Smiling at my sister from the passenger seat, I could tell that she was more nervous than I was about leaving me in the care of someone we had never met.

We were welcomed by a soft-spoken, blue-eyed woman and ushered into her nicely decorated home. The doctor introduced herself and, since she planned to work with me all day, made sure my sister was comfortable with the local area before telling her when to pick me up. In her protective way, Terry instructed me to call if I needed anything. Then she turned and left, leaving me alone with the doctor.

The doctor invited me into a comfortable, cozy sitting area to begin our meeting. Her opening words surprised me. "In our prior conversations, you said that you have forgiven your father, so I am going to ask you to call him right now and tell him you love him."

I was stunned. Knowing my father was not a man who spontaneously shared feelings, I felt a sinking in the pit of my stomach. My mind sought for reasons to deny the doctor's request. *How can I possibly make this phone call? Surely, my father will be confused, especially since he knows that I am calling from Florida!* Immediately, I prayed for strength and favor as I reluctantly took the phone from the doctor and dialed my parents' number.

"Hi, Dad," I said.

"Are you with Terry?" he asked.

"Yes, Dad. I just wanted you to know I am here and that I love you."

To my surprise, he answered, "I love you, too."

The doctor let me know I could end the call, so my dad and I said our good-byes. A seemingly simple conversation between father and daughter was not at all simple to me. Words of love from my father are a rare gift.

As we sat down to work, the doctor shared with me that she was testing the sincerity of my desire to heal. "You passed the test!" she exclaimed. She then began inquiring about my life's journey, uncovering important details about the painful relationships in my life. Every morning, she shared what the Lord had spoken to her in prayer the night before. With the Lord's leading, we would then discuss other significant relationships and events. For four days we discussed my first marriage, my parents, my sibling relationships, and my friendships.

We worked from morning through dinner, and the doctor graciously allowed me to cook my meals in her home. While going about daily tasks in the kitchen together, we forged a close bond, sharing our lives and our daily routine. At the close of each session, she often taught me relaxation techniques and helped me purify my spirit of any unforgiveness. It was amazing how cleansed I felt with each passing day.

That Wednesday, the doctor invited my sister and me to stay overnight with her and attend her class on healing at her church. We were delighted to do so, and Terry and I went out to dinner before the class so we could spend some time talking about the events of the past few days. When we arrived at St. John's Church, the doctor shared with the class why I had flown from Michigan to see her. Sharing openly, she explained that she had never before invited a total stranger into her home. "But, the Lord was clear with me that Laura was special, and we are working together to bring healing to her body, soul, and spirit."

Later, the doctor instructed us to break into small groups, and during that time a young woman with a prophetic gifting prayed for me in the hallway upon the doctor's request. Her gift was amazing as she revealed the secrets of my heart so delicately. I knew from my own training that this is exactly what the prophetic ministry should do. When our hearts are revealed, we are able to worship the Lord in spirit and in truth, just like the woman who met Jesus at the well (see John 4). As the young woman continued to prophesy, I fell into her arms and wept, and she said to me with authority, "Stop planning your funeral!" I had indeed been doing so. She told me to read the Gospel of Matthew every day for thirty days and spend time on my face in worship. I was deeply touched that evening and felt strengthened by this woman's kindness and gifting.

That night, my sister and I went to the apartment, and I rested while she read from a wonderful devotional. How healing and uplifting it was to share so intimately our love for the deeper things of God! My sister's devotion to me is something I will never forget, and I know that our week together changed me forever.

In the meantime, Jerry was keeping very busy back home. For years we talked about remodeling our bathroom and converting our attic space into a laundry room and closets. So, while I was away, Jerry arranged for our friend Matt to begin construction. His goal was to have the demolition phase complete and the space cleared and cleaned before my return home.

Jerry had expressed how much he missed me often during my week away, and he was anxiously waiting for me at the airport. While I was happy to see him, I felt apprehensive. Oddly, after such intensive work and honesty about my physical condition, I was hesitant to return and face the reality of my everyday life and the unknown aspect of what the upcoming months would bring. I wanted this ordeal to end, and I desired to have my life back!

Jerry sensed my anxiety and tried to help by showing me the room renovation. I looked at him, and with exhaustion and fear I said, "I hope I get to share it with you." His eyes filled with tears, and we quietly went to bed without much discussion. I have regretted my reaction and lack of enthusiasm, especially after being so encouraged in Florida. The Word reminds us that fear brings torment, and I allowed the spirit of fear to do just that!

I quickly drew upon a revelation God had given me when counseling others. He showed me in prayer that when we operate by our flesh, we put ourselves under the authority of the enemy. If we do not cast down thoughts that are not of Him (see 2 Cor. 10:5), our emotions become engaged, and our behavior follows their erratic pattern. Accepting thoughts that are not from God allows the enemy to gain control, and he then rules in our lives! We are cautioned in Micah 4:9: *"Now why do you cry aloud? Is there no king among you? Has your counselor perished...?"*

Using the principles and experiences I shared in this chapter, ask yourself the following questions:

1. Do I avail myself to the Father's Lordship by spending time each day in His presence? What can I change about my time with the Lord to open myself up more fully to the Spirit and return a more fitting offering of praise?

2. When making critical decisions, how do I distinguish between my fleshly desires and the peace that comes from walking as a son or daughter of the Lord?

3. Can I set aside the need for my child's approval in order to teach him or her to put away childish thinking and behaviors?

Chapter 6

A BITTERSWEET SURRENDER

No unbelief or distrust made him waver (doubtingly question) concerning the promise of God, but he grew strong and was empowered by faith as he gave praise and glory to God, fully satisfied and assured that God was able and mighty to keep His word and to do what He had promised (Romans 4:20-21).

GOD'S TIMING IS ALWAYS PERFECT, AND WHEN WE REMAIN IN prayer, we clearly see that it is so. While I was at physical therapy some months later, Ed quietly shared that he was actively pursuing and preparing for another therapist to join his team. By December, another physical therapist, Sue, was hired full-time. Praise His name for His faithfulness! Sue showed herself to be very sensitive to the Spirit and began assisting Ed with my care. Her help came not a moment too soon, for shortly after Sue was hired, I fell down four stairs. In pain and unable to walk on the treadmill, I was devastated that my activity level was affected once more, just as I was battling back yet again. But we would not be discouraged! I knew that the Lord's Mighty Hand had brought Sue into the picture.

Believing in His promises, Ed, Sue, and I began working very diligently as a team to reduce my pain and increase my mobility. My loyal therapists spoke life into my spirit, using their gifts to assist my body to do what the Lord designed it to do—heal. Looking me right in the eyes, Sue would tell me how wonderful I looked and what remarkable progress I was making toward my complete healing. When she spoke, I knew she believed what she was telling me. My body, soul, and spirit responded to the power of those words.

I had been off chemotherapy for over eight months. While it was a blessing to live without the side effects, the possible progression of the myeloma lurked beneath the surface, leaving me a bit unsettled. Fellowship and prayer kept me grounded. During one such time of fellowship, I was at home studying the Word with dear friends from church. We prayed and spent time edifying one another. My friend, Terri, began to ask some very heartfelt questions about the peace that seemed to accompany me through the storm. It was then that the phone rang—a constant reminder of pending test results and doctor appointments. It was, in fact, my oncologist's office requesting an appointment with me right away. Jerry was downstairs counseling and had just walked into the kitchen to get a glass of water. It was the end of the week, and he knew he could not get to the doctor's office with me until first thing Monday morning. My friend Becky spoke up and said, "I will take you!" I made the decision that waiting the weekend was not good for any of us, so I agreed to go with my friends, who would pray in the Spirit while I listened to the report from my oncologist and his assistant Danielle.

The bottom line of the meeting: I needed to begin chemotherapy immediately as my counts were in a dangerous place. Since I had promised my oncologist I would begin again if the report indicated I was headed toward a critical state, the plan was laid out before me. I was to have a bone marrow biopsy again the following week and begin the chemo regimen that very day.

Over the weekend, I began to prepare mentally and spiritually for the biopsy, and I knew that those results would coincide with the blood tests without any miraculous intervention. I was anointed with oil before my procedure, and with faith, I went to the hospital again to face Doc and the very long probe used to enter my bone marrow. At peace, I soon fell asleep. Before I knew it, I was awake and very sore. Unfortunately, the pain in my hip and leg increased over the following week, and it was discovered that the biopsy (one of many over the last two years) was done near the top of my hip, causing sciatica. I was unable to get around the house and had to remain sitting or lying down most of the day.

During therapy, the physical therapists worked diligently to move me, once again, toward healing. Unable to walk for even five minutes, I could not imagine ever being able to walk for fifty minutes, as I was doing before I fell down the stairs. With my love of physical activity, I was depressed about my inability to exercise while adjusting again to steroids and chemo. I felt forced to be alone and very still. Every movement and activity was painful and overwhelming. I lay awake one night in particular and tearfully begged for His mercy. Though my oncologist made it clear I needed the chemotherapy, my prayer was that Dr. Gonzalez would confirm this report. Scripture tells us in the Book of James that when we ask for wisdom without doubting, He is faithful to give it to us generously. Important decisions had to be made, and I did not want to make them without guidance from the Lord.

As soon as the biopsy results were available, Doc's office staff faxed the report of my biopsy and blood work to Dr. Gonzalez, and when he received them, the phone rang from his office in New York. "Laura, you have to start chemo right away. We are not holding this thing." In typical fashion, Dr. Gonzalez kept the conversation short and told me to stay positive and fight. "Stay on your program and keep your immune system strong. Your body will correct itself at some point, Laura." *When? When, Lord?*

I hung up the phone and stared into space, trying to figure out what feelings were manifesting underneath the numbness. I hated to think about daily injections of blood thinners and high doses of steroids on top of the Revlimid.

My friend, Nita, called that evening and asked, "How's your head?" I knew exactly what she meant and began to explain that I was disappointed, but ready to fight again. Like a true friend, Nita dug deeper. "How's your heart?" I looked at Jerry, who was sitting with me in our bedroom, and the tears began to flow. I drew strength from his eyes as I searched my soul for words to express how I felt at a deeper level. *Search my heart, Lord! I am clinging to the hope that is within me, but I am growing weary. Desperation threatens to darken my spirit, but I must hold fast and speak life for my family as much as for myself. Let your lamp shine, Lord, that I might walk through this present darkness!*

It is interesting how my perspective on the battle changed over the course of the journey. I waited until I was able to write to everyone regarding my need to begin chemotherapy yet again. I was devastated that I would have to share disappointing news once more, as everyone knew I stood in faith that I would not have to do so. Oh, how I wanted the miracle to manifest itself at this juncture! One thing about close friends is that they, like the doctors, become overwhelmed by the demands placed upon them by my battle with cancer, particularly the emotional demands.

As always, Pastor Loren's message was prophetic and just in time! The Lord was faithful to address the need to stand, despite the negativity we receive from those walking in the flesh. He reminded us that we must not look at the circumstances around us, but we must look only upon the promises made by the Father to us! We left the service feeling renewed and refreshed, ready to stand in our increased faith.

I started chemotherapy and the blood thinning injections right away. How I hated beginning the routine of medications again! It grieved my heart to watch Carmen give me the injections. I know it took courage to do so day after day, piercing her own mother's body in the hope of healing.

Though I adjusted to the Revlimid, the combination of steroids and chemotherapy caused forgetfulness. I fought hard to keep active by exercising daily with my walking sticks. The steroids kept my white count up, so I was able to attend church regularly, and my spirits remained stable. Remarkably, my tumor markers dropped significantly within two months, which was a surprise to everyone. I was responding to the drug!

During my course of treatment, I became confused at times, and one night my memory lapse was devastating. I was upstairs in the new laundry room washing some delicate blouses in the sink, while Jerry was in his office counseling a client. I turned the water on to fill the sink, and without thinking, I left the room. I completely flooded the laundry room and Jerry's closet. I was so frustrated with myself and so upset that I had caused Jerry this kind of trouble. He came up from counseling late that night and immediately began to drill holes in the kitchen ceiling downstairs because the water had seeped into the roof. He did all he could to save the drywall and then put down buckets and fans. A few rooms were damaged because of my forgetfulness. I was not myself. Ashamed and despairing, I could not control my tears.

I have had other bouts of forgetfulness caused by the chemotherapy, but the magnitude of this incident drove home the concept of being a burden in a profound way. As each day passed, I fervently prayed for wisdom so I would know when it was time to break from the therapy. It was important, according to the specialist we saw in Buffalo, to take chemo "holidays" and allow the body to restore and rebuild the immune system. From a medical perspective, multiple myeloma is an unending battle, making it necessary to design an individual's protocol creatively.

With wisdom from the Lord, I followed the way of peace and made the decision to continue the Revlimid for one more month. My blood levels were at a safe point, so I wanted to give the medications another cycle to lower them one more time. My target date was to stop mid-July and then begin a period of watching and resting.

As the markers showed stability, I completed the last cycle and began my journey off of the drugs. Within a week or two, I noticed some throbbing in my right ankle. I immediately attributed the pain to my walking regimen and assumed that the discomfort was due to the damage in my vertebrae. I had complained of sciatica after my bone marrow biopsy the previous February, and since then I just assumed that the sciatic nerve had been hit during the test. Unfortunately, the MRI performed one month later in March did not include the sacral spine, so I was left without a definitive reason for the ankle pain and sciatica.

We went out to dinner for Carmen's birthday in July of 2008, and I remember bringing a footie sock along to keep my ankle warm at the restaurant. Each day afterward, the throbbing pain in my ankle became more intense. Unable to get comfortable, I resorted to taking pain medication to relieve the symptoms.

The following Thursday, my friend, Mary, stopped by for a visit. She took one look at me on the couch and realized that I was not doing well. An occupational therapist herself, Mary runs a clinic at a local hospital and works in conjunction with many medical disciplines. Her knowledge and instincts are good, and she put them into action, quickly deciding to take me to the physical therapy clinic to see Sue. The energy work done there would help my body relax and heal more efficiently. Mary also wanted another set of eyes to evaluate my condition.

I could no longer hide my pain, and it soon was out of control. Screaming in agony, I managed to lie on the treatment table with help from my friend and the physical therapist. Mary sat very close to me, watching the physical therapist's hands work to bring relief. Like a mother hen, my friend wanted to be sure the method of therapy was appropriate for my condition. Sue, my therapist, looked at me and calmly said, "Laura, I am going to do my best to relax you, but there is a level of pain that requires assistance from medication." Before I realized what was happening, Mary was out the door and on her way to collect my pain medication from home. I was unaware of the time that had elapsed and again, Mary was at my side with water and pain pills. Within an hour, Sue finished her work, and Mary was able to get me back into her car. Knowing that I could not be left at home alone, she put me into bed and made sure Carmen was aware of my condition.

The next morning, I slowly got ready for my day when the pain began again. Still focusing on the assumption that I was having sciatic nerve pain, I employed a technique my husband taught me to take pressure off of the nerve in order to bring relief. His research on sciatica indicated that lying over a pillow would help, but as I lay there, the pain became so intense that I again began to scream and could not get up. Thankfully, a young man from our church, who had been our houseguest for a couple of months, was with me at home and came to my room to help. He was one of Carmen's friends and was active in our young adult ministry at church. He was staying with us for a time to regroup, and we were happy to provide a home and support during his transition.

When he saw my condition, he called Carmen at work and explained that I was again in crisis. He calmly handed me the phone, and I was relieved to hear Carmen's voice. Carmen quietly asked me to explain what was happening, and I cried out to her for help, begging that she take me to the emergency room for a steroid injection to relieve the pain in the nerve. Reacting quickly, Carmen began collecting her things, but asked me to stay on the phone with her until she left the office. "Hang on, Mom. I have to make one more phone call, but I want you to stay with me. Just hang on."

While I followed Carmen's instructions, she used all the God-given authority she could muster and contacted my oncologist's office on the other line, informing them of my condition and seeking direction. The doctor told Carmen to take me to the emergency room for a Decadron injection for pain, and then he instructed her to bring me to the office for an evaluation.

As soon as I received the shot and felt some relief, I was ready to go home and rest, so I promptly got up from my bed in the emergency room and told Carmen and that I was ready to go. Hoping to get back home quickly, I was dismayed when Carmen took a wrong turn, so I asked her where she was headed. With boldness and determination, she informed me that we were headed to the oncologist's office to determine the appropriate action moving forward. In my stubbornness, I tried playing the "mother card" and sternly told Carmen to take me home, insisting that I was fine and did not need to be examined.

Carmen's friend, who had remained quiet in the back seat, retorted with some humor, "Mama Laura, this is not a party you get to R.S.V.P for!"

When I realized Carmen was not going to follow my direction, I again told her that I had no time to wait for an appointment, and if the office was busy I was not going to stay. Deep inside I dreaded waiting in Doc's office when things were not going well. My thoughts were racing as I attempted to prepare myself for his evaluation and decision on the matter. I had not received good news in a long time, and it was stressful to feel as though some unknown disaster was always looming over my head.

When my oncologist came into the room with Danielle, his assistant, he began asking questions without ever sitting down. It became clear that they were after information in a hurry. Doc looked at me, shaking his head, and queried, "Which toes are numb, Laura?"

I remember feeling perplexed, but then I suddenly realized that I did indeed have numbness in my toes and the outside edge of my right foot. I never paid attention to it, which was not uncommon for me. The sixth of eight children, I became used to staying quiet unless I was in a crisis. Though my mother took good care of us, there was always a lot of activity in our house with eight children. Developing a high tolerance for pain came naturally from my father, and I carried that same personality into my experience with cancer. After answering Doc's questions in the affirmative, an MRI was scheduled for the next morning.

Mornings used to bring hope and excitement of things to come. But too many of my mornings brought uncertainty and fear, and I felt a sense of dread as we headed for the hospital. Carmen waited in the reception area as they took me into the radiology clinic. Before I knew it, the test was over, and a familiar face came into the room as I sat up on the table.

"Laura," a kind man named John spoke gently to me with concern in his eyes, "your case seems familiar to me. Have I worked with you before?"

"Yes," I replied, recognizing him and reading his concern. I then recapped my history briefly.

John put his arm around me and with gentle conviction said, "You are a strong woman."

I shared with John that I knew my life was miraculous and that I had a strong faith in God's willingness and ability to heal. He encouraged me to continue believing and helped me to the waiting room to find Carmen. As I walked with him, I knew the medical report was not good, but there is a relief in being able to name your enemy. From experience, I knew in that moment, with the wisdom of the Lord, that we would pray for a miracle, formulate a plan of action in preparedness, and execute upon direction. Knowing that "greater is He that is in me, than he that is in the world," all things are possible (see 1 John 4:4).

Within an hour of my return home, the doctor's assistant called Carmen with the report. "We know your Mom doesn't like hearing these things, but there is a tumor on her sacral spine, and it's wrapped around the sciatic nerve. She has to go to the hospital right away." Knowing the drill all too well, Carmen contacted Jerry and packed my clothes for the hospital. We were once again being thrust upon our own road to Calvary. *Why must my daughter be the one to help me carry this cross?* My mind was spinning and everything was a blur.

In a fog of disbelief, we headed to the hospital again for my third surgery in two years. The staff bypassed my admission process at Carmen's request, and I was wheeled directly to my room. Before I even had time to process all that was happening, an I.V. of Decadron was running through my veins to reduce the swelling from the tumor, protect the spinal cord, and reduce the pain. It did nothing for my pain. As a result, Delaudid and Oxycontin were immediately added to my regimen, along with a Morphine drip. Immediately, plans were in place to begin radiation, and mapping was scheduled for the next morning. The hospital staff recommended that I be transported by ambulance for the radiation treatments each day for one week, until I was able to go home and continue the treatments on an outpatient basis.

Much to my surprise, Joseph, a minister from the church, and his wife arrived as I was getting settled in my room. I breathe a sigh of relief whenever the saints of the Lord come to pray! In my weakened state, the Spirit of Christ within them was a lifeline for me. Joe anointed my head with oil and began to pray in the Spirit, looking directly into my eyes with such a strong conviction and power. He prayed in tongues, which were different than I had heard before, and they came from the heart of the Father. I felt immediately transported with Christ into the Garden of Gethsemane, and His presence was powerful around me.

The wonderful thing is that He joined me in that place. There was a unity of spirit like I have never before experienced. It was a profound moment that I will never forget because I believe it symbolizes God's plan for the Church—a corporate healing which will manifest itself through an incredible unity among His saints. It is when we become one with Him that we will become a mighty, united army of God, willing to go to that place with one another.

The next day I was transported by ambulance across the street to the radiation oncology center for mapping. I kept trying to advocate for myself with the doctor, but was having a difficult time articulating. I wanted to discuss the possibility of Cyberknife treatment, a new technology in radiation therapy that protects surrounding tissue. The doctor told me firmly that there was no benefit to this kind of therapy given the characteristics of myeloma and the type of tumor I presented, which had tentacles wrapped around the sciatic nerve originating from the sacral spine. Again, I had to trust God to give the doctors wisdom to orchestrate the best plan for me. Feeling helpless and out of control, I surrendered to the loving and faithful arms of my Father. *Your hand is upon me, Father, keeping me from harm. I know You are near.*

Doc met me early the next morning on his rounds, and with an air of authority he informed me that intravenous chemotherapy was necessary once again. "We are running out of wiggle room," he stated firmly.

"How do you know that?" I asked.

Doc began to tell me that if a tumor was on the sacral spine, he was certain there were others.

I was in no mood for theories, so I told him to prove it to me. "Let's do an MRI of the spine!" I demanded. I was not about to be denied. It was a clash of two strong wills.

The next morning, Doc called me from home and agreed to an MRI. I relaxed knowing that we could never go wrong with more information, and I was not about to make any decisions based on fear and assumption.

By the time the EMS technicians brought me back to my hospital room later that day, I was delirious with pain, and the sound of guttural screaming could be heard from my room. Holding on to my leg, I begged for someone to help me. My parents and three sisters—Roseanne, Barbara, and Ann—came to see me just as I had been put into my bed. The scene brought my parents to tears. As they clung to one another in desperation, my sister, Roseanne, who is also a nurse at the hospital, immediately headed for the nurse's station. With determination and a strong protective instinct, Roseanne got the attention of the Head Nurse on duty, and a more effective plan was put into place for pain management.

I kept pleading with no success, "Get Mom and Dad out of the room!" I didn't want my elderly parents to see me in such a vulnerable and traumatic condition. It was so very painful to see the suffering in their eyes as they watched me cry out in pain. How it grieves a parent to helplessly watch a child suffer! Not wanting to see my mother and father in such anguish, I decided that I would never again ask them to visit me at the hospital.

Within minutes, I was given more pain meds and soon was unaware of my surroundings for the rest of the weekend. Though dazed, I began to experience feelings of betrayal. I could not comprehend how my blood work showed improvement, and yet a tumor ominously hid behind the effects of the steroid, waiting to rob me of my vitality and hope.

My sister, Elvie, came that Saturday to see me, as she was in town for a wedding. It seemed every time she came home from Arizona, I ended up at the hospital or in some physical crisis, and I was thankful for her time, love, and prayers. Through family and friends, the love of Christ poured forth yet again, and each day brought more support and encouragement from the Body of Christ. Pastor Loren and Bonnie came after church, and I wept as I shared my heart. How exhausted and full of confusion I was at that moment! Yet, as much as I wanted to be done with this jour-ney, my burden for those in captivity was greater. We held hands while praying in the Spirit together. Visits from others filled the room with the presence of Christ, and I was blessed by Fred's musical gifting as he played his anointed violin for me. As the Word states, *"How beautiful...are the feet of those who bring good news..."* (Isa. 52:7 NIV).

During my hospitalization, heavy doses of pain medication caused hallucinations, and I somehow am able to recall a few of them. At one point, I remember thinking I was running on the track where I worked out years before. Carmen said that I instructed her to get the pizzas out of the oven and told her to be careful not to burn herself! In my stupor, I later asked my sister Ann to "tell all those women to get out of my kitchen!" When she asked me to explain, I shouted, "They're trying to make lasagna, and they don't know what they're doing!" It is a good thing to laugh, and apparently I gave my family plenty of opportunity to do so!

Monday began my first day of radiation treatment. I awoke early to do my makeup and hair before the EMTs came to my room, still having enough fight within me to care about my appearance. I was a bit emotional about being transported to radiation, and the whole experience left me deeply saddened and vulnerable. I choked back tears as they wheeled me down the halls to the outside, sickened and in pain every time we rounded a corner.

Carmen got in the ambulance with me, rubbing my arm and dispensing my pain medications at specific intervals as instructed. With my sister Roseanne's assistance, we were able to keep me pain-free during transport the entire week. As we reached our destination and they lowered my gurney from the ambulance, Carmen and I saw one of my myeloma buddies, Raoul, from my oncologist's office. Raoul was failing in health, and I had been very concerned and saddened about his condition. He was being wheeled ahead of me for an appointment, so Carmen asked if I wanted to see him. I quietly shook my head and wept bitterly. I missed laughing together and supporting each other as we had done in the infusion room time and time again, but the spirit of death was all around me, and I could not bear to see Raoul failing. As much as I had resisted being part of the world of chemotherapy, I quickly became part of the "family" of patients at Doc's office. Raoul died four weeks later.

During my hospital stay, I continued to grieve the fact that my body had betrayed me. Again, I asked myself, "How could my blood work have looked so good and yet a tumor was lying in wait to overtake me?" The tumor was a stronger clone that resisted the Revlimid, just as the tumor in my neck had done two years prior. When Pastor Loren and Bonnie came to visit and pray, I mentioned that I was thankful for one thing: If I had not gotten off the chemotherapy and steroid when I did, the tumor would have continued to grow, its effects masked by the drugs, and it could have caused damage to the spinal cord.

It was humbling and touching to wake up and find Carmen's friends sleeping on the cot next to hers. Each morning brought another precious face full of support, love, and provision. Christopher faithfully arrived each day with a wonderful home-cooked meal and reassurance that he was taking care of everything at home. He wept next to my bed one night, weary from the stress of my illness and wanting life to be "normal" again. There was no time to process what was happening, and we were keenly aware that, at a moment's notice, life could take a drastic turn in an unknown and devastating direction. I recalled how Jesus spoke to Peter and said, "Peter, there will come a day when someone will gird you and take you to a place you do not want to go" (see John 21:18). Again, we were on that dark, narrow road of suffering and surrender.

After being discharged from the hospital, my family accompanied me each day for outpatient radiation, and by the second week, I began to have bleeding and diarrhea. I could hardly walk, and I became weaker and weaker, losing weight daily and suffering severe pain from the burning radiation to the sacral spine. My voice was very weak, and the nights were long. Jerry begged me to take the pain medication, but I was determined to tough it out. I would wail and cry out each day, but as Jerry handed me the meds, I shoved them back at him, determined to resist them. Taking narcotics went against everything I believed. For years I had never even taken an aspirin, and I was fearful of being forced down a road I never wanted to take. It was all too much to endure. My coping skills were limited, and it required incredible endurance on Jerry's part. Day after day, he hung on to me and cried by my bedside as he prayed and calmly but firmly convinced me to take the Oxycontin.

During the radiation, we noticed what appeared as a burned area of skin extending from the spine around the front of my body and covering my abdomen. The itching became unbearable, and the electrical shooting pain was excruciating. What we attributed to the radiation ended up being shingles that went undiagnosed. My fever reached 104 degrees, but I was too sick and weak to even consider a trip to the doctor's office. Not having the presence of mind to think beyond the moment, I fell off to sleep from exhaustion.

Jerry had already arranged for a week of vacation time at home, so the timing was perfect for him to care for me after completing radiation. I was too ill to allow anyone else to care for me, as he had to lift me into the tub every day and provide total care. I remember being so weak I couldn't see his face when he lowered me into the water. I was so thankful for the time we had together. With loving care, Jerry made all of my meals since I was too sick to make it down the stairs. When he wasn't directly caring for me, he spent time repairing things and working around the house. The only thing he did for recreation was take a bike ride in order to get some exercise and a fresh perspective. A real vacation—a time of complete refreshment—was a distant memory for both of us.

Jerry and I talked and decided that he should take Melissa, Chris, and Carmen to dinner, just to give them a chance to talk, laugh, and reconnect as a cohesive unit. It has always been important to us to remind the kids that we are there for them as parents. Even when life is unpredictable, as it certainly was at the time, our love and dedication remain consistent. I remember being so happy that they would all have an evening together, but deep inside me was a sadness that I couldn't be with them. Torn by the mixed emotions, I couldn't help but wonder if Jerry was preparing the kids to go on without me. It was very bittersweet.

Christopher had an especially hard time leaving for dinner without me. His countenance gave him away, and we inquired about his feelings. With a sensitive thoughtfulness that I have always loved about my son, Christopher shared with Jerry and me that he was afraid the dinner plans would make me feel that I was not a significant part of the family anymore. I knew he had been fighting back tears for days, wrestling with feelings of betrayal and grief. With our encouragement and reassurance that the outing was a positive thing for the whole family, Chris agreed to go.

One of my sisters came to the house to care for me so that Jerry and the kids could relax at dinner without worry. While at the restaurant, they all had a wonderful time together. Jerry, in his wisdom, encouraged a sense of humor and fun and just let all three kids talk. Able to relax and enjoy a very good meal, they were renewed by their time together. The evening brought a sense of cohesiveness that often gets destroyed during crisis. It had been over two years since I came out of remission, and we could see each one of our children working tirelessly to keep the household running while standing strong in faith. As counselors, we were keenly aware that it would be easy to lose sight of their relationship with one another and with us while working hard to remain standing. Having counselors for parents has its benefits, depending on the perspective, but we are who we are, and we operated comfortably from that place.

When the week was over, Jerry fervently prepared meals ahead and cut up all of my carrots and vegetables for juicing. I had no strength to push the vegetables into the juicer, so he had made provision for the entire week. I could see the worry on his face as he prepared to leave me alone and return to work. I choked back tears as well, scared to death to navigate life without Jerry at my side at all times. Trying not to panic, I used every ounce of self-control as we approached the end of Jerry's week at home.

Every day was a victory, regardless of the fact that progress was seemingly nonexistent. I passed the night hours by singing unto the Lord, truly experiencing what the Word of God calls a "sacrifice of praise." Speaking life, health, and restoration to my body took every ounce of strength within me, but I was determined to fight. I could hear Jerry praying with me in the darkness, as he rarely slept for fear that I would fall while trying to walk to the bathroom. A walker was placed next to my bed, and I shuffled slowly several times per night.

One night, while Jerry was still on vacation, and after removal of the tumor on my spine, I was screaming from the post-surgical pain. It was two o'clock in the morning, and I told Jerry, "Please call Mama Jean." He hesitated at first, afraid to wake my dear spiritual mother in the middle of the night. In a firm voice I demanded, "Get on the phone and call Mama Jean, and she will pray with me." Mama Jean, Pastor Loren's very own mother, had told me on several occasions to call her no matter the time, day or night. It was unlike me to take her up on the offer, but at that moment I had to believe she meant what she said. Her gifts of healing and compassion were everything I needed. Mama Jean had prayed with me every morning, and she always declared healing and victory to my weary body, soul, and spirit.

Sensing the depth of my need, Jerry quickly picked up the phone and dialed her number. Mama Jean prayed until I fell asleep, and like the Good Samaritan, she did not stop with her first effort to help. The next morning she called to tell me that she stayed awake after praying with me and contended with the Lord, pleading my case before Him. "I believe you are going to come out of this valley, Laura. Enough is enough!" What a servant's heart!

The following Monday, Jerry left for work crying. My heart sank as I felt his pain. As a caregiver, he had to watch me suffer, knowing he could not stop the cancer from causing more agony. To this day, Jerry is a fierce protector, but even he could not prevent the hurt. The tears streamed down his face each night as he lay next to me in prayer.

I rarely let my emotions take over, not wanting the kids to see me vulnerable and broken. However, one morning as I was getting ready for the shower, I cried out in desperation, "I hate my life!"

Christopher, who always stays protectively nearby in his room while I shower, heard me screaming and said, "I know, Mom. I know."

I wailed, not knowing how I could possibly go on anymore. For three months before the diagnosis of shingles—August through October—I lived with severe pain in my back and abdomen, having no idea of its source. The pain was so intense. Like Job, I cried out through my fear and desperation, unable to understand the will of God. *Why, Lord, must the climb become steeper in my darkest hour?*

When circumstances occur that result in our dependency on family members for our care, we can become vulnerable to a mentality of victimization. One of the manifestations of this syndrome is entertaining thoughts of being a burden to those assisting us. This can lead to a relationship of indebtedness and responses propelled by guilt. Our motivations must be brought into the light in order to live as pure vessels equipped to overcome everything that hinders our mature walk.

I spent each day in prayer, listening for the voice of the Father to guide me and waiting upon Him to heal. I felt led to arrange a trip to New York to see Dr. Gonzalez and discuss the need for any possible changes to my enzyme therapy program. In October of 2008, Marilyn and I boarded a plane for LaGuardia Airport. Thankfully, my dear friend, Mary Anne, again offered her apartment in the city and provided a car, so all of the details were handled without worry. Upon arrival, we ordered dinner and went to bed so we would be ready for my appointment the next morning.

When we arrived at Dr. Gonzalez's office, I was immediately at peace, as always. After spending so much time, day after day, literally dragging myself from one sterile environment to another, it was reassuring to be in an atmosphere where every effort is made to fight disease naturally. I knew, even though the myeloma was waging a formidable war, Dr. Gonzalez would work hard to fight with me every step of the way, keeping my body and immune system in the best possible working order. It was humbling for me to see Dr. Gonzalez in my present condition. After so many years of remission and good nutritional support, I presented myself in a sickly condition for the first time. My face was disfigured from the steroids, which affected my adrenal glands and caused Cushingoid symptoms, and many bedridden months left me struggling to walk. My one little victory: after all of the chemotherapy, I had not lost one strand of hair! Since I had stopped chemo in July, I never expected what was about to happen in the coming weeks.

My test results in New York showed that my body was indeed trying to correct, and Dr. Gonzalez remarked that the scores were miraculous. In the calm before yet another storm, my mouth praised God for His continued faithfulness to heal me! Did He not promise to be faithful every step of the way? What a reminder that He indeed goes before us in all things!

Although it had been several weeks since my hospitalization, the shingles and the side effects of radiation left me battling for my strength once again. Finally able to control the diarrhea with medication, I made plans to go in and have my port flushed. At the time, this procedure did not raise any unusual level of concern, even though my first convulsive episode occurred immediately after Roseanne accessed my port to provide hydration while I was completing my last round of radiation a few months prior. I was quick to assume that the radiation had caused the convulsions, and I was too tired and weak to think more about it. Little did I know that this episode was soon to repeat itself.

After returning from New York, Marilyn took me to the doctor for the port flush as planned. Afterward she said, "Let me take you out to eat and get you some soup." Knowing I had little appetite, Marilyn wanted me to try to eat something soothing. So I sat there at the restaurant, and within the hour I began to shake. Concerned, Marilyn looked at me and said, "You are not just cold; there is something wrong." The waitress noticed me shaking and offered to help us out the door. From there, Marilyn walked me carefully to the car and started the seat warmer. It was impossible for me to speak because I was shaking so hard, shivering uncontrollably. When we got to my driveway, Marilyn left me in the warm car, ran inside, and prepared a cup of hot tea so that I could drink something comforting as soon as I got in the house. She called Jerry, and he came right home. It took one hour for my body to stop shivering, and I was weak and sweating profusely. Wondering what could have triggered this reaction, I assumed that a missed dose of Oxycontin sent me into drug withdrawal. We did not call the doctor, and in my weakened state, we made a faulty assumption that could have cost me my life. How merciful God is that He covers us in our mistakes! Is He not the sovereign One who is Lord over the heavens and the earth? Is anything out of His grasp or authority?

The whole episode left me exhausted and weak, and I was unable to go anywhere outside of my room. Exactly one month later, after my port was flushed once more at the doctor's office, I had another similar episode. My symptoms were so severe that I had to be admitted to the hospital again. Finally, the infection in my port was diagnosed as klebsiella pneumonia, which had been contracted when my access line broke during hospitalization for the tumor. The infection had gone undiagnosed for so long that it spread to my bloodstream, and I felt so very ill that I feared I might not recover. The nurses came in regularly to check on me while I lay staring. There was no motivation to listen to music or teachings. I was weak in my body, and my soul was weary from the road. At night, while lying in my hospital bed in the dark, I sensed a blanket of death falling over me. Even Doc and the nurses, not used to seeing me deathly pale and disheveled, thought I had given up hope. But I had not. *"Even though I walk through the valley of the shadow of death, I will fear no evil, for You are with me..."* (Ps. 23:4 NIV).

Day after day, I lay quietly in my hospital room as the hours slowly passed. I felt buried somewhere deep within my spirit, and I could not help myself. The Word of God echoed within me:

> *...Unless a grain of wheat falls into the earth and dies, it remains [just one grain; it never becomes more but lives] by itself alone. But if it dies, it produces many others and yields a rich harvest* (John 12:24).

My tolerance for blood labs all day long and throughout the night wore thin. I wasn't sleeping due to the constant interruptions, and I was drained. To make matters worse, after three attempts by different nurses to reconnect my I.V. one day, my sister, Roseanne, came to my room after work to check on me. I shared with her that three nurses tried to insert the needle without success, and I was feeling a bit frustrated. In her very experienced and calm manner, Roseanne found a vein near my wrist that she could feel but not see. She explained to me that she knew she could tap the vein and wanted to know if I trusted her to do so. I relaxed immediately because I knew she was going to get the job done. Roseanne inserted the needle and tapped the vein with success. With precision she then anchored it beautifully, and it did not slip out or cause a problem for the rest of my hospital stay. She was my treasure sent by God at that moment!

Frustrated by the length of my hospital stay (which was about a week long) and the constant poking, prodding, and testing, I turned to Jerry while he was at my side and said, "I'm checking myself out of here! Do you hear me?"

I watched as Jerry tried not to smile, seeing that familiar twinkle in his eyes that told me he was aware of my irrational thinking and knew it was not wise to respond. He squeezed my hand as the tears rolled down my cheeks.

Shortly after I found out that I would not be released for several more days, my dear friend and pastor, Jeanne, was at my side when I needed her most. I complained vehemently to her. She responded calmly, "Laura, did you understand what the doctor said?" I just looked at her and answered with resistance. She continued, "You have to stay, Laura. It is better to take care of the infection so that you don't have to come back. You need to settle the fact that you have to be in the hospital for a while longer." Jeanne always spoke with a compassionate authority, and I could not argue. Truthfully, I wanted to scream, but I again submitted to her leadership with a bit of resistance in my spirit. I could not get out of this prison fast enough!

Though we may have to surrender to the care of our physicians in a crisis, the words we speak in times of frustration must never succumb to the taunting of the enemy and come out as negative confessions. Our words create our world! Truly, through our words, we have the power to create an atmosphere of victory and healing rather than one of defeat and despair. In moments of overwhelming anxiety and emotional stress, we have to strengthen our resolve in the Lord, adjust our thinking, and choose to *speak* life. First Samuel 30:6 keys in on this principle, when David faced incredible opposition: *"David was greatly distressed, for the men spoke of stoning him because the souls of them all were bitterly grieved....But David encouraged and strengthened himself in the Lord his God."* We must do the same!

As the days passed slowly in the hospital, I was greatly encouraged by every visit from friends and family. Each visit brought glimpses of home. One day, my pastor came to see me. Despite his busy schedule, he patiently sat with me as we talked about offering up my suffering to the Lord, knowing that He was doing a very deep work in my children and my family. I shared with Pastor Loren that when I was in my greatest pain, I wept and said, "Lord, how did You handle it during the crucifixion? How did You ever make it through?"

I shared with Loren that I had gotten frustrated, and he replied, "Laura, I know that you love the kids enough to allow this process to take place for their calling." And I knew, though I swallowed hard, that I did.

Tears were in my eyes as I processed my pastor's message; he left, and I pondered his words the rest of the day. They were words for one who is willing to "lay down her life" in order to leave a legacy that could not be left any other way. *Am I really willing, Lord? Am I mature enough to let all of my plans and dreams go for the sake of my children's callings?* He comes as a refiner's fire to scrub away our carnal nature so that His likeness is left for His purposes. "Greater is He that is in me, than he that is in the world" (see 1 John 4:4). Did I realize that this journey would be a purification process developed through fire? Every layer of my fleshly nature had to be peeled away so this vessel could be fit for the Master's use.

My dear friend, Bonnie, came to see me on Saturday, and with enthusiasm and love, she brought the Word of the Lord. No matter how brief or long my visits with Bonnie, they are always full of meaning and life. As she sat by my side, she shared that the Lord had spoken to her and reminded her of the story of David and Goliath. David had approached Goliath with nothing but his faith to defeat him. With boldness, David faced the giant before him and declared:

> *You come against me with sword and spear and javelin, but I come against you in the name of the LORD Almighty, the God of the armies of Israel, whom you have defied. This day the LORD will deliver you into my hands, and I'll strike you down and cut off your head....* (1 Samuel 17:45-46 NIV).

Bonnie then shared a word that had been spoken over her, which declared that her hands were hands of healing. We believe when the Lord declares a thing, and so Bonnie, Carmen, and I all agreed together as we prayed for healing. Bonnie laid her hands on me and began to speak life over me. Woman to woman, Bonnie knew the sadness and humiliation I felt because of the changes in my physical appearance. With comfort in her voice and compassion in her eyes, she put her arms around me and said, "You're okay, Laura, you're okay." Those words of life always sank deeply into my human spirit. Somehow, I knew everything would be okay and that the tender prayers of the saints covered me.

After what seemed like an endless hospital stay, I was finally discharged with orders to continue intravenous antibiotics at home. As we pulled into the driveway, I was in awe of how lovely my home looked. Somehow, the path leading to the front door seemed ethereal as I saw my precious dogs, Hunter and Delaney, wagging beside Jerry to greet me. I wept humbly, so thankful to be alive, and I walked around my kitchen as though it was my first time seeing it. How lovely to have a place to call home! How beautiful to be greeted by my family and surrounded by the calm and peaceful spirit that was present there. Chris held me as I walked upstairs to my room to change. "I'm so happy you are home, Mama. It is so good to have you with us. It is not the same without you." Each moment passed as if I was living in slow motion. Every nuance was held in my mind as though captured by my memory.

I was not prepared to learn all the intricate steps for hooking my line to my I.V., but the process soon became routine. Three times each day, I flushed my port and ran the antibiotic through a Huber needle that was placed within it. We were finally getting the infection under control, and I started to feel more alert every day. I even tried to go up and down the stairs, pushing myself for one more flight, one more time, just to gain some strength. Oh, how I would pray, crying out in the middle of the night for months: *Lord, comfort me in my distress; bring healing and strength to every fiber of my being! In You alone is my hope for victory!* Despite me being so ill from the infection, we received a glimmer of hope when the doctor called with the latest MRI results. "Your MRI is fine. You have no other tumors, and your blood work shows that your tumor markers have gone down." *Glory to God! May His strength quicken my mortal body!*

I was again reminded of the difference between happiness and joy. When life crumbles around us, His joy pours over us like a river of life, healing, and hope! Day after day, I struggled, trying to gain strength and keep fighting. I could no longer continue in my own abilities because I had little strength left. Staying in the presence of the Lord and being naked in my empty state before Him brought an outpouring of His grace and mercy, which I was blessed to share with others. One night in particular, I remember receiving a call from my friend, Lynne, a faithful intercessor with whom I have prayed for years. As we lifted our hearts in prayer, the Spirit of the Lord just fell upon me, and somehow I knew that I had touched the heart of God. We prayed for one another. Because of the economic downturn, Lynne's husband, Gary, had relocated out of state to secure a job. She was learning to cope with the loneliness, as she could only see her husband on the weekends. Having been cared for and prayed over by so many for so long, I was blessed to be able to minister to my friend in a time of need. Boldly, I cried out for her and carried her burden before the Father.

In time, the long-term effects of chemotherapy, combined with the steroid use and the epidurals I received to treat the pain from shingles, resulted in the loss of my one remaining physical victory—my full head of hair. To a woman, her hair is her crowning glory, and I had asked the Lord to please let me keep this one physical attribute that had not been affected by the cancer and treatment. But, with fourteen times the normal amount of steroids rushing through my system causing Cushingoid symptoms, it was only a matter of time before the drugs won out and had their way with my body. I became so very depressed. The last vestige of my womanly appearance, the one remaining physical characteristic that anchored me to my past and gave me hope for the future was slipping through my fingers, literally. But the Lord was clearly calling me to anchor myself in His Word alone, seeing only His image and surrendering the "me" that I always saw myself to be.

If it were not for the Body of Christ, my suffering—both physical and emotional—would have left me in a helpless state. I remember one day in particular when my humiliation and physical pain were more than I could bear. Ann's three daughters, my nieces, were raking leaves in my yard to raise money for their upcoming retreat. Julia had just come in the front door as I was struggling to get into my lift chair at the top of the stairs. I was weak and moving very slowly, and my eyes met hers. Julia, in her very mature and discerning way, read my face like a student intent on learning her craft. She hastened to the top of the stairs, and without a word, she wrapped her arms around me and just held me, whispering, "It's okay, Aunt Laura. I love you." It took all the strength within me not to fall apart in her arms. *She's only a teenager, Lord! I don't want her to be afraid for me!* With tears streaming down my face, I thanked her for her sensitivity. By God's grace, I let go and allowed His strength to take over in that moment. Had I not done so, I would have melted into a heap on the floor.

Julia and her two sisters, Jenna and Maria, are precious to me, and their love and encouragement continually support me through some very difficult times. Maria, in her usual fearless way, frequently crawls right into bed with me, wanting to be of help under any circumstance. And I will always hold dear a letter I received from Jenna as I was grieving the loss of my hair and my physical strength. In the letter, Jenna shared that I am her role model of strength and perseverance, and she reminded me of her faith in my healing. In my darkest hour, when I feel like giving up, I remember my obligation to my young nieces—my desire to set an example of tenacious faith—and I keep fighting.

While everyone's life experiences are different, there comes a time when we all encounter tribulation on some level and are faced with a choice to either strengthen ourselves in the Lord, not wavering on the promises of His Word or the conviction that He is *always* good; or lose heart, lose hope, and give up. I encourage you to go before the Father, rehearse the rich promises of the Word in light of difficulty, and reflect on the following questions:

1. What does *surrender* look like to me when I am in crisis? Can I continue to operate with the authority of the Lord, undergirded by the conviction that He is always good, even when it appears that everything is out of control, or do I completely surrender by giving up?

2. What, in my understanding, is the difference between travailing before the Father's "throne of grace" and speaking negatively about my circumstance to those who have no power to change the circumstance? In which manner have I operated in the past?

3. Do I have a clear revelation and understanding of the creative power of my words? If not, how can I be more mindful of the impact of my words on my own well-being and that of those around me?

Chapter 7

GRACE, GRACE

Bless (affectionately, gratefully praise) the Lord, O my soul; and all that is [deepest] within me, bless His holy name! Bless...the Lord, O my soul, and forget not... all His benefits—Who forgives...all your iniquities, Who heals...all your diseases, Who redeems your life from the pit and corruption, Who beautifies, dignifies, and crowns you with loving-kindness and tender mercy; Who satisfies your mouth with good so that your youth, renewed, is like the eagle's [strong, overcoming, soaring] (Psalm 103:1-5).

THE HOLIDAYS WERE DRAWING NEAR, AND I WAS THANKFUL TO be out of the hospital and off of antibiotic therapy just prior to Thanksgiving Day. Needless to say, my holiday spirit was definitely waning. Having been isolated in my bedroom from August through November, I knew that it was probably a normal depression or sadness that had come over me. In the past, before my battle with cancer, my heart and soul went into every holiday detail, from the decorating and baking to the homemade gifts and festive gatherings. Holidays at my house always looked like something out of a picture book. But this time, this year, was different. I knew that everyone would be home for Thanksgiving—Christopher and Carmen, along with Melissa, Bryan, and the grandkids. But it was all I could do to just put one foot in front of the other. I grieved not being able to act on my passion to cook and provide a nice holiday for my husband and children.

Once again, my friends and family came to the rescue! Taking over my kitchen like a crew of elves, my friends, Becky and Wendy, along with my sister, Roseanne, began preparing and freezing food for Thanksgiving dinner using my recipes and organic foods. Because of their graciousness, all we had to do was take the food out and thaw it. As we gathered around the Thanksgiving table together, I realized that all the shopping and typical holiday fanfare meant nothing to me; I just wanted to be with my husband, children, and grandchildren. What a blessing, and what a perfect reminder that the things for which we should be most thankful are not "things" at all!

After coming out of remission, a prophetic word spoken over me by Jerry was now beginning to manifest. The word the Lord spoke to Jerry was that I would begin to see the significance of the number five working in my life as the days progressed. As I studied the Scriptures, I learned that there was numerical significance in the Hebrew alphabet, and that the number five represents grace! Beyond eternal salvation, I began to experience a new side of the Lord as my Abba Father, my Daddy.

As Christmas approached, I couldn't help but wonder if it was going to be my last, even though I clung to the promise of my healing. Somehow, kindred spirits in the Body of Christ always seem to know when I most need encouragement, and this holiday season brought many special surprises. Ed, my physical therapist, sent his daughter Stephanie, an interior designer, to my home to decorate a tree for me. In casual conversation, Ed and I had talked about the holidays, and I remarked about the beautiful tree in his office. The next thing I knew, his daughter Stephanie arrived, and there was an exquisite Christmas tree adorning my home! It shimmered with golden light and was unlike any tree I had ever seen. It looked like something out of a whimsical forest, and I could see the joy that it brought my family and everyone who came into my home during the holiday season. Christmas carols echoed through every room as the youth group came to sing for us with leaders from our youth ministry. The gift of their presence was very humbling, but very edifying at the same time. To top it all off, Lisa, one of my dear friends from church, secured tickets for us through her family business, and we were able to see *White Christmas* at the beautiful Fox Theater. As the lights lowered in the theater that night, tears streamed down my face, and I thanked the Lord for such precious moments with my family. Even though I was physically drained and emotionally spent during the holidays, the Lord clearly revealed that He cares about the very details of our lives. What gentle care our great and gracious Lord uses to write upon our hearts and heal our brokenness!

In early December, Christopher and Carmen left for a missions trip to Peru. Since every day was a struggle for me, I looked forward to receiving their e-mails because news of their trip breathed life into my spirit. As I read them to my husband, I wept. *Praise the Lord for all He was doing in their hearts!* Their inspiring messages were the greatest gifts of the holiday season.

Christmas Day was upon us, and I was happy to be invited to my sister Roseanne's house for the family celebration. Relieved of the usual details and planning, my heart was to just enjoy the kids. Melissa had gone to Arizona with Bryan and the grandkids to visit Bryan's family, so the day was quiet but restful. I found that it all worked for good because I needed to rest and didn't have the energy for much activity. I was in extreme pain Christmas Day, and it took every ounce of concentration just to stay focused through the fog of pain meds.

It was a larger than usual gathering since my sister, Terry, and her family came home for the holidays. In the back of my mind, I wondered if they made the trip because they wanted to be sure to see my ailing mother and me. Given my battle with cancer and my mother's struggle with Parkinson's disease, each day is tenuous for my family. As I prepared to leave for the family gathering, I struggled with whether or not I had the strength to go, but I wanted to see everyone and knew it would be good for us to attend.

Jerry, always at my side to protect me from falling, waited with me in the foyer for my sister, Roseanne, to come and pick us up on Christmas Day. As I walked to Roseanne's car, I was feeling very conscious of how I looked, especially since my hair was falling out more and more every day. I looked at Jerry and tearfully cried, "I'm ugly!" At that, I fell into his arms and wailed as Jerry wept quietly. I think I just needed to get it all out, and part of me felt like such a disappointment to myself and to everyone who had been fighting this battle alongside of me.

Faithfully, Jerry just kept repeating, "It doesn't matter; it doesn't matter. We love you, and more than anything, we have compassion for what you're going through."

Jesus nailed sickness, disease, and condemnation to the cross, unleashing the power of grace into the world. In the heat of a battle, the multifaceted nature of His matchless grace manifests. When we fall on our faces—naked before Him—willing to exchange our weakness for His strength and the power of the fulfillment of the law, the manifestation of love is made known in our atmosphere.

Christmas Day seemed to lift the burden and help heal the pride in my physical appearance—a false pride that I didn't want to surrender. From that day we began to notice that my hair was growing back, producing little hairs underneath the long strands that were very sparse and flyaway. At the same time, we were preparing mentally for a number of upcoming medical tests. Following through on my promise to my oncologist and Dr. Gonzalez, I scheduled an MRI, a bone survey, and a bone marrow biopsy for the second week in January. We also scheduled adrenal testing, which thankfully confirmed that no tumor was evident on the adrenal glands.

Something struck me as I wrote to Jeanne, my pastor and counselor, and updated her on my schedule of medical tests and the feelings I experience before undergoing each and every one. In her written response, Jeanne shared how much it spoke to her that I submitted to the process of the testing. That statement was so affirming. It penetrated deep within me. I never saw my willingness to undergo medical tests as a demonstration of submission. Somehow, Jeanne's declaration affirmed my willingness to choose to fight this battle, though I could have chosen to quit at any time. It reminded me that the Lord had done a work in me, and as much as I hated the whole process of testing and waiting and wondering, He was working a trust and maturity in Him as I faced the giants before me.

I approached the New Year and the week of testing with great resolve. After the bone survey, I was exhausted and in pain from lying on the hard table. A tear rolled down my cheek, not just from the pain, but also from the emotional wear and tear that the whole process of testing brings. Then the technicians brought me into the MRI department and helped me onto the table for the next test, which we had set up on two separate days so that I would not have to receive general anesthesia for three hours. Dr. Gonzalez and I had discussed the testing ahead of time, and he felt that it was best to not undergo anesthesia if at all possible. As my body made its way into the MRI machine, I had a panic attack and couldn't breathe. I told the technician that she would have to get me out.

When I spoke to Dr. Gonzalez about it and shared that I was also having difficulty breathing at night, he reassured me that the shingles play a huge role in inducing panic disorder. So, after much searching, we found a facility that provides the Wide Open MRI, and we scheduled my appointment for the following Sunday. The machine was like a huge hamburger bun, and after lying on the table they slid me between the two sections. The hardest part of the test was having my arms extended and locked in place over my head for a while as they obtained images of my thoracic spine. Despite the discomfort, I was happy that they could complete all the images in one evening. The following Friday was my appointment with my oncologist to discuss test results.

On Thursday, the anxiety caused butterflies in the pit of my stomach. I purposely scheduled my biopsies that same day so that I could attend church service the night before, where Mama Jean anointed me with oil, and I was built up in my faith during the communion service. When Mama Jean laid hands on me to pray, the presence of the Lord fell so strongly that I could hardly move. She looked at me and said, "Laura, did you feel that? Did you feel the presence of the Lord? It was so strong!"

And I answered, "Yes!"

Minutes later she came back to my seat and said, "Laura, the Lord wants you to know to expect a better report."

How I wanted to believe her words! *"Lord, I know Your will is healing!"* Nevertheless, I confess that the anxiety and butterflies remained, and as the day approached for my appointment, I felt like I was going to pass out. It took every ounce of prayer and concentration, allowing the Lord to remind me of His promises. *What can man do to me? Nothing can separate me from His love!*

I asked the Lord to prepare my oncologist's heart, his words, and his reactions to me. As we sat in the waiting room on Friday, Doc passed through, approached me, and whispered in my ear, "I have good news for you today." Oh, I wanted to scream and praise the Lord! When we went into the examining room, Doc asked me to stand up and said, "Read the report, Laura." And there it was—a plasma cell percentage of 5 percent! The pathologist had noted that there was improvement in my bone marrow, as well. My beta two was normal, and my albumin had increased. What a blessing! What a miracle! Even my doctor asked what was in the water I was drinking. I told him it was Jesus and shared with him my experience. Though he skeptically listened, his reaction did not phase me. I knew that God was planting seeds, and I knew what God had done.

What an atmosphere of rejoicing in our home! The kids were so relieved; I could see it on their faces. In the weeks that followed, I worked every day at strengthening my core, trying to sit and stand for longer periods of time. Slowly, I continued the process of weaning myself off the Oxycontin, one-half of a tablet at a time. The physical withdrawals were inevitable—the sweats and the emotional ups and downs. But it was all worth it, for the house was again filled with the laughter of my kids and their friends, and oh, we began to feel life in a way we had not experienced in a long time! We even rejoiced in every curly, small strand of hair that grew in place of the old! *I know that I am walking in a new day, and it is time to walk out the work that You have put in me, Oh Lord!*

All along the way, through each victory and setback, I faithfully follow Dr. Gonzalez's treatment program. None of the expenses are covered by insurance, and Jerry works very hard to supply the funding needed to purchase my pills. While in prayer one day, I asked the Lord if He wanted me to continue the program. The burden for my husband was great, and I wept deeply before the Father. Within just a few minutes after I prayed, the phone rang. I answered, and an employee of the warehouse that distributes my enzymes replied, "Laura, this is Jill from Nutritional Services. We are aware that you have to take a large number of enzymes. How are you doing?"

"I am in a battle with cancer," I explained, wondering why she was calling.

She continued, "We had a return order from a patient, and we are unable to sell the unopened bottles of pills. You were on our hearts, and we would like to donate them to you." At that moment, I was in shock and could not contain my tears. I shared with Jill that I had just been in prayer and that her call was miraculous! It seemed that the year 2009 held great hope, and I pressed forward in faith.

Hope is something we cannot afford to live without. Hope is more than a casual "wish." In fact, true Biblical hope *(elpis)* is "the joyful expectation of good."[1] In times of chaos, confusion, and struggle, we have to be confident that our Father is near to our weakness. He is good, and therefore, we can fall before His feet, exchanging our weakness for His strength, with the full assurance and hope that His promises are sure. Take a moment to reflect on your own life experiences with these questions in mind:

1. When have I freely exposed all of my weaknesses before the Father? Is it time to humbly bare my fears and my failings to the One who understands me the most? Do I let pride get in the way of the restoration that He has in store for me?

2. Do I see God as "high and lifted up" when I go before Him in truth?

3. Am I aware of the danger of hiding my pain, weaknesses, and vulnerabilities before God? If not exposed before Him, to whose lordship am I submitting?

ENDNOTE

1. James Strong, *Strong's Exhaustive Concordance of the Bible* (Peabody, MA; Hendrickson Publishers, n.d.), s.v. "Elpis," #1680.

Chapter 8

A DEEPER WORK

You have also given me the shield of Your salvation, and Your right hand has held me up; Your gentleness and condescension have made me great (Psalm 18:35).

IN LATE 2008 AND INTO EARLY 2009, JERRY AND I SPENT TIME with one of our pastors, who has her doctorate in counseling and has always maintained a close relationship with us. It was a very good meeting, and we were able to share much about where we were on this journey. It was painful to hear Jerry's heart as he described a recent discussion with Carmen, where she had asked him for advice about something and declared, "Papa, tell me what to do. You can fix everything!" I knew that her words hit Jerry deep within his human spirit. Listening to him share his feelings touched me in a very deep place, and each of us was able to identify ways to encourage one another in the midst of this trial. Again, the Body of Christ is a well of healing and strength, and we were energized and renewed when we left the meeting.

God's timing is always perfect because later on that evening Dr. Gonzalez called to inform me that my January blood work was inconsistent with the biopsy. He asked me to have my oncologist's office fax him February's blood work. After receiving those results, Dr. Gonzalez called again and indicated that the IGG (immunogammaglobulin) proteins—the tumor markers—had risen even farther. After discussing the blood work, we decided to take a "wait and see" approach because the results of all the other recent tests—MRIs, scans, total body survey, and biopsy—were so miraculous. In an e-mail message from Jeanne, she affirmed our decision by exclaiming, "We are going to watch this, and I'm pressing into God like never before!" In her encouraging way, Jeanne reminded me to stay focused and reassured me of her prayers and love.

Sue, my physical therapist, was making frequent home visits to work on my back. Definitely gifted in her work, Sue cares for the whole person and always reminds me that tears are very important because they contain a chemical that releases toxins from the body. If we fail to release those toxins, we are in greater physical pain. So I have learned to let myself cry on occasion just out of shear frustration, while standing in faith knowing that God has not removed Himself from this situation. My pastors continually remind me to release my need to reason things through because God is in control. And so, I watch and wait on the Lord, knowing that the Lion of Judah must come to deliver and restore me.

I became ill with bronchitis shortly after our meeting with Pastor Jeanne and was prescribed antibiotics again. The infection caused a lot of coughing, which stressed my weakened ribs and dislocated some of them. Toward the end of my course of antibiotics, I began to run a fever and woke up one morning feeling very strange and chilled. My temperature was 100 degrees, so I knew I needed to see Doc right away. Jerry and I arrived at Doc's office as quickly as we could, and within a few hours, I was admitted to the hospital once again. I wept, knowing that I would miss the inaugural opening and dedication of our new sanctuary at Mt. Zion. The dedication was something I had waited for and longed to see. Doc's assistant reassured me that if I was doing well enough, they would give me a pass to return home for the service.

Jerry and I were so sad that I had to go into the hospital again. After getting me settled in my room there, he returned to work, leaving me alone. Carmen had just received a promotion and was working late, and both kids were extremely busy rehearsing for the inaugural dedication service. On her way home from work that day, Carmen insisted that she stop by to see me, even though she had rehearsals that evening. I would not allow her to do so, and she wept. I tried to protect her. Still acting on my instincts as a mother, I continue to protect her to this day. Unfortunately, I ended up having a very severe chill while at the hospital that day, almost a convulsive type like the one I experienced four months earlier when my port was infected. The extreme shivering was traumatic, lasting almost an hour. Sure enough, it was another infection in my port—the same bacteria that was found in November. Intravenous antibiotics were administered immediately, and my fever broke that night. I was relieved when my friend, Lynne, arrived to visit and pray with me. She has been my prayer partner for years, and her words comforted me as she rubbed my leg and softly prayed. Feeling weak and exhausted, I was so very grateful for her visit.

The psalmist writes:

He delivered me from my strong enemy and from those who hated and abhorred me, for they were too strong for

*me. They confronted and came upon me in the day of
my calamity, but the Lord was my stay and support. He
brought me forth also into a large place; He was deliver-
ing me because He was pleased with me and delighted in
me. The Lord rewarded me according to my righteousness
(my conscious integrity and sincerity with Him); according to the cleanness of my hands has He recompensed me*
(Psalm 18:17-20).

The Lord is working a deeper work in me to this day. Recently,
several very sad things happened to people that we love, and it was
revealed that our loved ones needed our attention and God's gentle
touch. In affirmation of all that was being revealed, one of my
dear friends called me and said, "Laura, more than ever when I
left your home, I see that your home is set apart. It is truly a safe
place." She shared just how rare it is to be ministered to in a safe
and peaceful environment. Continuing to pour out her heart, she
explained that safety brings such healing, and she shared that she
had begun to pray for us and thank the Lord for Jerry and me,
releasing herself in praise, which was so very freeing.

After she shared these thoughts with me, I recalled a word
the Lord had spoken to me last summer: "Laura, your house is
a light set upon a hill for all to see, and they will come and hear
the Word of the Lord." The Lord reminded me of what it is to
be a sanctuary—a sanctuary for His Spirit. A sanctuary is place
of peace, righteousness, and rest. The Lord continued, reminding
me of how many, many years ago I had asked Him to build me a
house. At the time, I was grieving over the fact that we had sold
our home in the country when I was first diagnosed, knowing
that my medical program would be costly and we would need
every extra dollar to pay for Dr. Gonzalez's care. As a result, we

had to move to an unfamiliar place, as if we were starting all over again. I pleaded, "Lord, just find me a home!"

He answered and reminded me of how He even chooses the places where we shall live! And over the years, even though my heart ached and grieved when we left our country home, I now see the work that the Lord has done, strategically placing us in this home near the church, because many have come for healing. Living so close to our church has made it convenient for others to stop by when they are hurting and in need. As I pondered these things, the Lord gave me the Word that he had given David when David wanted to build a house for the Lord. Patiently directing His servant, the Lord commanded, "No, *I* will build *you* a home." I see now that, in our life together and in our marriage, the Lord has taken Jerry and me and lifted Himself up, for the Lord has said, "If I be lifted up, I will draw all men unto Me" (see John 12:32). And truly, He has been lifted up in Jerry and me as we have died to our flesh and become more and more like Him, walking in His ways.

I understand that the Lord is building His army and that all the work He continues to do in Jerry and me is meant to be a legacy for our children. In First Chronicles 17:8-10, He says:

And I have been with you wherever you have gone, and I have cut off all your enemies from before you, and I will make your name like the name of the great ones of the earth. Also I will appoint a place for My people Israel and will plant them, that they may dwell in their own place and be moved no more; neither shall the children of wickedness waste them anymore, as at the first, since the time that I commanded judges to be over My people Israel. Moreover, I will subdue all your enemies.

Furthermore, I foretell to you that the Lord will build you a house (a blessed posterity).

This Word of the Lord has inflamed our hearts, and I see that Jerry and I are called to be a sanctuary, and that we might walk worthy of that calling. I do not have time to be sick anymore. More than ever, I see people hurting, crying out for help. Like the prodigal son, they are weary and ready to turn from darkness. Like the benevolent father, Jerry and I run to them, our hearts desiring to bring restoration and healing.

When we are going through a dark night of the soul, our willingness to avoid becoming self-consumed produces a greater measure of wisdom in guiding others toward healing and victory. The heart of ministry to the Body of Christ is a desire to see others become greater than the vision we have for ourselves. Discerning the timing and degree of that assistance is vital in prayer, so our capability to provide is weighed in wisdom.

Nine glorious months passed as I continued to pray and seek God for my healing. Working hard to detoxify from the chemotherapy and pain medications, I quickly lost twenty pounds, and my face began to lose the swelling. I became accustomed to life off of medication and was feeling like my old self again. Before long, however, I began to notice discomfort in my right shoulder, and when my doctor's assistant, Danielle, called and told me to make an appointment to see her at the office, I knew my proteins were rising. Danielle was firm about my need to begin therapy, so a bone marrow biopsy was scheduled. It was so hard to tell the kids. We all stood together and cried, but we agreed we would not let the disease dictate our response. Again, I grieved going back to "Chemoland," knowing it would force my family to adjust to another personality change on my part.

Desiring affirmation from the Lord in all of our decisions, Jerry and I met with Pastor Loren. When Loren prayed for us, he explained that we were entering a season in which God would work His perfect love in us. Loren told me that the veil was going to be removed, and I would see the Lord face to face. I knew we were again being taken down the dark road that would bring a deeper knowledge of Him and a change in us. Turning back before leaving the room, Loren said to me, "Laura, there is one more chapter for you to write. It will be on love, the First Corinthians 13 kind of love." I surrendered my heart right there, but I knew this was not going to be an easy road.

Immediately, I began to study God's love, and every day I read the text in First Corinthians 13:

> *Though I speak with the tongues of men and of angels, but have not love, I have become a sounding brass or a clanging cymbal. And though I have the gift of prophecy and understand all mysteries and all knowledge, and though I have all faith, so that I could remove mountains, but have not love, I am nothing. And though I bestow all my goods to feed the poor, and though I give my body to be burned but have not love, it profits me nothing. Love suffers long and is kind; love does not envy; love does not parade itself, and is not puffed*

up; does not behave rudely, does not see its own, is not provoked, thinks no evil; does not rejoice in iniquity, but rejoices in the truth; bears all things, believes all things, hopes all things, endures all things. Love never fails. But whether there are prophecies, they will fail; whether there are tongues, they will cease; whether there is knowledge, it will vanish away. For we know in part and we prophesy in part. But when that which is perfect has come, then that which is in part will be done away. When I was a child, I spoke as a child, I understood as a child, I thought as a child; but when I became a man, I put away childish things. For now we see in a mirror, dimly, but then face to face. Now I know in part, but then I shall know just as I also am known. And now abide faith, hope, love, these three; but the greatest of these is love (NKJV).

As the days passed, I kept hearing the Word of the Lord echo within, "I am your exceeding and great reward." How I searched my heart in prayer over this truth! Was He indeed my greatest treasure? Would I willingly lay everything down for His sake? My focus for so long had been on all of my deficiencies, and I was uncertain about how this next phase of my life was going to play out. What did God have in mind for me now? In my thinking, I could never be good enough to receive healing in my body. I wanted to be whole more than anything, and yet I was cautious to check my heart in my pursuit of it. I struggled to fully understand and live the Word that Pastor Loren had advised me to study in First Corinthians 13:9-10:

For our knowledge is fragmentary (incomplete and imperfect), and our prophecy (our teaching) is fragmentary (incomplete and imperfect). But when the complete and perfect (total) comes, the incomplete and imperfect will vanish away (become antiquated, void, and superseded).

The morning of the biopsy I was emotional, and tears rolled down my cheeks as I entered the procedure room. My pastor's mother, Jean, gave me a miracle cloth, and I clung to it as the anesthesia took effect. The following Monday, I received an unexpected call from my oncologist. He informed me that my bone marrow results came out better than anticipated, with my plasma cells at eight percent, and he asked me to reschedule my appointment for Thursday so he could think. When we met, Doc agreed that we were on the border with whether to begin therapy, and we discussed all options. We concluded that we were still headed in the wrong direction with my proteins, and that the cancer was not going to stop moving. After much lively discussion, we all agreed that it was better to begin treatment while I was still strong. Jerry and I talked more over the weekend and called the office the following week, informing them that we wanted to begin a light dose of Revlimid three days per week. It was our hope to arrest the spread of the cancer.

As I was praying with the intercessors for the nation during our Saturday prayer service in May, Pastor Loren approached me with a Word from the Lord. Laying hands on me, he prayed, "Father, quicken her mind to see the Word in this day. The enemy is coming against her, but Lord, you will cause Laura to see herself from Your perspective. She will speak the Word and defeat every giant that has come against her."

As Pastor Loren was finishing, Lolly, an elder in the church, also approached me to pray. "Lord, the same Spirit that raised Jesus Christ from the dead dwells within her and will quicken her mortal body!" The Word of the Lord is life and healing to my spirit! I felt so blessed that the Lord cared so deeply to minister to me at that moment. How my spirit leapt with joy, as I was ready to do all things through Christ in whose strength I walk!

It was the summer of 2009, and we continued down this path until the pain in my shoulder and arm became unbearable. I was shocked to hear that another set of x-rays showed no change in my condition, so I insisted on a PET Scan, and the results indicated severe involvement of the cancer to the humerus in my right arm. The radiation oncologist stated that the entire area was "mottled," showing "punched-out" lesions with only spongy material remaining. Radiation for two weeks was ordered in light doses to regain use of the arm and promote healing in the bone. Since I was having trouble sleeping on my right side, the ribs were given electron therapy, which was effective immediately.

Upon completion of the radiation, more tests were ordered to identify possible myeloma involvement in my thighs and pelvis because I was unable to walk without a cane and needed answers. The results were sobering. There was a large lesion on my right femur extending up the hip, a lesion on the sacral spine affecting a nerve, and a smaller lesion on the left femur. It was decided that I would consult with my oncologist to determine whether or not another intravenous drug should be added instead of more radiation. Expressing concern over the risk of fracture to my femur, the radiation oncologist advised us to prepare our home for the time when I could no longer walk or climb any stairs.

When I returned home from my appointment, I noticed a dozen red roses at my door with an attached card. As I opened the card, I was amazed by the love God had poured upon me again! The note was written by a fellow intercessor from church, and it read:

Laura, God is getting ready to unveil His masterpiece in you. The work He has done is almost complete. He has numbered the days for your remembrance. You shall look back and see the hand of your creator designing you for perfection.

I immediately called the woman to thank her for her kindness and prayers. We had met officially for the first time on the Fourth of July. Since then, she felt led to pray each day for me as directed, and after one month of seeking the Father on my behalf, He spoke the Word that she shared with me in her note. Humbled by the Lord's leading, she told me that He directed her to buy the roses.

She asked Him, "Why, Lord? I hardly know Laura."

He replied to her, "I want her to see herself in the natural as I see her."

I wept as my fellow intercessor sensitively shared this message from the Lord. She would never have known the painful thoughts and feelings I have brought before the Lord in that secret place regarding the loss of my physical health and appearance. My once athletic body was gone, and the deformity in my rib cage was so uncomfortable and ugly to me! How tender the mercies of our Savior, who sees and knows all things before they are ever spoken!

Though Doc wanted to begin I.V. chemotherapy right away, he listened intently to my plea to give the Revlimid more time to work. I had responded to this oral drug very well in the past, and I did not want the complications of a port at this time. He agreed to give the current protocol a chance and decided that we would assess the results in a month. Cautioning me, however, Doc echoed the concerns of the radiation oncologist regarding the lesions in my leg and hip. He did not want to risk a serious fracture.

During that meeting, I presented Doc with another challenge. I shared with him my desire to attend a Notre Dame football game in South Bend, Indiana, with my father. Since my dad is a Notre Dame alumnus, home football games are special times for him. At eighty-three years of age, my dad was undergoing many changes in his own life. My mother was no longer able to live in their home due to the advancement of her Parkinson's disease. After my mother had many falls, my sisters called a family meeting, and it was decided that our youngest sister, Ann, would take Mom into her home to care for her. Plans were put into place to begin construction on an in-home apartment at Ann's house so that Dad and Mom could be together. The impending sale of their home, which they had lived in for over forty years, left Dad saddened. I knew, given my illness, that I needed to make a memory with him.

Doc was reserved about the matter and left the decision to Jerry and me. Jerry was very nervous about the trip. Though he agreed to go, he expressed concern about my condition and the toll the trip would take on me physically. I immediately put a plan into place that would make Jerry feel more comfortable and help lessen the chance of injury. A wheelchair was prescribed for my comfort and safety, and a letter was sent to the university ticket office requesting special stadium seating so I could sit in the bleachers comfortably. Everything was in place so I could spend the weekend with my father, along with Jerry and our daughter Melissa.

While Doc was doing his best to accommodate my wishes, what I did not know was that he had spoken with Carmen and told her that I should not be left alone at home. Knowing that I was in need of constant assistance and care, Carmen was having a difficult time dealing with the pressures of her recent promotion at work. Though God provided help with my meals and transportation to doctor appointments, Carmen's heart was to be with me.

Carmen requested a meeting with her boss, and arrangements were made for her to take a leave of absence. The relief on Carmen's face was remarkably apparent, and she immediately embarked on a plan to keep the household running smoothly while caring for me every day and helping me avoid as many trips up the stairs as possible. Her maturity and dedication amazed me, and I marveled at her sense of priority in her life. At twenty-three years of age, I am not sure I would have chosen to forego a promising career to stay home and care for my mother with such grace.

With Carmen's assistance at home, we were able to enjoy breakfast or lunch with Melissa and our dear friends on occasion. These outings allowed me to stay intimately connected to the relationships in my life. Though it was difficult to maneuver with my physical challenges, I wanted to know what was happening in the lives of my friends. Sickness can confine us like a prison door, shutting out every possibility of being a light to those around us. Knowing I was incomplete without connecting to the Body of Christ kept me reaching out and taking in every ounce of the Lord's breath of life through each and every person.

Making memories with my children and seeing them set new priorities in their own lives was a gift, as well. Melissa, Christopher, and Carmen had to look deep within to stay anchored to the Father and understand His calling for each of them individually. Melissa began to feel emotions she had never before allowed herself to feel. The pain she experienced in her past had created a barrier in her own relationships, and she wept as she described the beautiful revelation of becoming a drink offering to those around her.

When we are ill or going through difficult times, the temptation to hide the truth from our children exists because of our natural instincts to protect them. We must apply prudence in communicating bad news according to their age and emotional maturity. Studies show that children of all ages will form conclusions through the personal lens of their life experiences. These conclusions can result in an exaggerated sense of reality and can impede coping skills. God's timing is perfect, not our own timing. Therefore, we must pray and seek wise counsel before sharing details of our struggles with our children. Full transparency is useful only when the truth is shared in love and received with adequate understanding.

Though I would have chosen to be healed long before, I began to see the importance of waiting on the timing of the Lord in all things. After all, the work He was accomplishing involved many in the Body. *Am I willing to walk humbly and accept that Your timing is perfect, Lord?* I was not always certain that my body could take anymore, but somehow His love was very thoroughly rebuilding me. My crumbling skeletal system was standing by the gentle craftsmanship of His ways and truth.

As I continued to reach out to others in whatever way possible, they continued to pour into my spirit. I received another note from my friend Judy:

My Dear Sister Laura,

Your healing *is coming* and it isn't as far off as you might think. Praise God! I see breakthroughs happening! It has been so many years that this thing has taken such a tight hold in your body, but its stronghold is being diminished daily. Deliverance and complete restoration are coming. Praise Him! You are such a precious sister in the Lord! Praise Him!

Love, Judy

I was determined to continue fellowship with my friends and attend church services, although the challenges of nausea and exhaustion made it difficult. I even became a regular at a new restaurant with my dear sisters in Christ and enjoyed their companionship. Though it would have been easier to stay in bed on occasion, I returned home refreshed and ready to face each day, having drawn strength from my relationships with the seasoned women in my life.

Mama Jean continued to pray with me each day and left messages on my voicemail to encourage me, sharing the Lord's command that we were not to give up. I saved every voicemail message that spoke life unto my spirit. Words of life are "health and healing to the bones" according to the Word of God, and I took each message seriously.

By early September, I was fighting the battle of increased physical pain. The Oxycontin was difficult to tolerate because it made me react to things with greater intensity than normal. I shared with Pastor Loren that I felt as though I were in a fish bowl or reality show, especially when Carmen's friends erupted in laughter at some of the odd things I would say. Certainly, I wanted Carmen to have her friends around as much as possible, but I was often embarrassed by my reactions to things. Pastor Loren and Mama Jean persuaded me to "have fun with it." Their encouragement gave me liberty to accept myself and enjoy the journey. What power we have to bring freedom to one another by our speech!

Pastor Loren instructed me to come to the altar every Wednesday so he could lay hands upon me for healing until we saw improvement. I told him I would willingly run to the altar for healing! How precious to be in a house that believes in the power of healing! What a gift to have a shepherd who seeks the Lord on behalf of his sheep!

One Sunday, I visited with Leta, an elder in our church who had mentored me for years in prophecy and intercession. After chatting with her for a while, I got up to return to my seat. Leta suddenly asked me to sit down again and began to pray and prophesy over me. "Daughter, the joy of the Lord is your strength. His hand is upon you for good and not for evil, and you will go to the nations and speak the Word in the days ahead." I thanked Leta for sharing the prophecy and walked back to my seat, so grateful for the Lord's care over me. My spirit was encouraged and soaring!

To this day, I am determined to stay in church and attend intercessory prayer on a regular basis, even when the side effects of chemotherapy are unbearable. I do my best to minimize the side effects by detoxifying my liver regularly and continuing my enzyme therapy program. It is vitally important that I maintain enough physical strength to get to church as often as possible. The Word of Life brings healing to my spirit, soul, and body, something the medicine can never do.

I have come to realize that we are coming to a place where we truly understand the life of the Word of God. One particular Wednesday, I spent the day in prayer and travailed before the Lord regarding the ongoing decomposition of my skeletal structure. In my sadness and grief, I tearfully questioned the Lord. *What are You doing here, Lord? What is Your plan?* Struggling to walk and needing a cane, I was undone again. *Isn't the unbearable pain enough, Lord? Just look at my body; I am far from the active person You made me to be!* Had I not let go of my love for exercise and athletics? I became keenly aware that I held disdain for what had happened to me physically, and that I was ashamed of my deformed rib cage and rounded shoulders, which overcompensated for the lack of support in my neck and spine.

After our midweek service that evening, a young man named Scott, whom Jerry and I mentored, approached me. "I have something to share with you, Laura, and I really don't know why the Lord wants to tell you this. I have been fighting the Lord for two weeks about coming to you, and He said I had to speak with you tonight." I looked at Scott with curiosity, and he continued with calm assurance, "You will exercise again!"

There it was, simple and revealing! The Lord had truly heard my cry, and once again He showed Himself merciful and compassionate in my pain. I must have appeared shocked by what Scott said because his eyes filled with tears. The word caused me to bend over and weep before him. "You don't know what you just said to me!" I cried. Scott not only had no knowledge of what occurred in my time of prayer that day, but he also had no knowledge of my background in athletics.

The 24th of October 2009 finally arrived, and we left in style for the football game in South Bend, Indiana. Melissa's husband, Bryan, provided a comfortable car for transportation, which was helpful in preventing pain in my spine. We settled into our hotel room and took Dad out to dinner at an Italian restaurant. It was so nice to visit with him, and afterward he took us on his traditional guided tour of the campus. Jerry held on to me as we lingered behind, watching as Dad showed Melissa his old dorm and told her the story about "Touchdown Jesus." We then went to the basilica, where I sat in the pew to rest while Jerry and Melissa toured the beautiful surroundings with Dad. What incredible architecture and art! Melissa was mesmerized by the experience. Dad later walked us to the Grotto, where we said a prayer and lit candles with him for our families as a symbol of our faith.

Walking around the Notre Dame campus at night was like touring a village in Europe. The lanterns, old trees, and charming buildings were beautiful, and it was a peaceful experience. I was amazed by Dad's ability to find everything in the dark, but he knows the campus like the back of his hand. As a student at Notre Dame, he found a sense of family and faith there, and he wanted to share his love for the university with all of us. Many of my childhood memories are centered on Notre Dame. We spent time there whenever we were in the Chicago area visiting relatives, and Dad often brought home sweatshirts for us as souvenirs. To celebrate my parents' fiftieth wedding anniversary, our whole family—over thirty of us—stayed in a dorm together for the entire weekend. We gathered in the chapel, where each one of us presented special memories and favorite moments with my parents. The weekend culminated in a wonderful dinner, renewal of their wedding vows, and a surprise dedication of a bench on the campus near the Grotto. Dad visits his bench and sits on it during every trip to the campus.

Game day brought rain, but I was determined that my prayers for good weather over the previous month would not go unanswered. While riding on the shuttle, I respectfully but boldly told the Lord that rain was not what I requested! When we got to the stadium, Dad snapped my rain poncho around me and made sure I was going to be dry and warm for the game. I stood patiently and allowed my father to take care of me, just as he did when I was a child. All of the vulnerability from childhood was present with a security and love that was deeper and more profound than I had ever experienced. This level of love was a choice; I was now willing to let my father take care of me, unafraid of the hurt from the past. At that moment, we both were aware of the brevity of life and the power of love to heal and restore. The differences in our faith did not matter at that moment because life had taught us lessons that could not have been learned any other way. That memory with my dad will forever be with me.

Allow me to back-track and shed some light on the events that led to restoration with my parents. In February 2006, I received news that my mom had been diagnosed with Parkinson's disease. My sisters had been taking turns sending my parents meals, as my mother could no longer cook on a daily basis. Though I was experiencing severe pain in my spine, I wanted desperately to join my sisters in support of my parents' needs. I always valued caring for my parents, and my heart had not changed, even though my father refused to see me. I finally saw them in April of the same year, as my Uncle Albert had just passed away. I wanted to bring flowers to my mother, knowing she was grieving the loss of her brother. Only two weeks before I received the news that the cancer was everywhere in my body, I visited my dad and mom, attempting to restore our relationship after three years of separation. Then, in May 2006, when they received a visit from my sister, who informed them about the seriousness of my condition, my mom and dad quickly made arrangements to see me, as I was in bed, full of tumors and racked with pain from broken bones and the cancer. Since that time, God has been so faithful to make a way through all of our disagreements and misunderstandings, and I am thankful for the moments that I have with my parents.

By the time we sat down for the game, the rain had stopped. And, by the end of the first quarter, the sun was shining! Not only was God faithful in providing good weather, but He also made sure there was no one sitting behind me. An empty seat was a rare occurrence at a Notre Dame football game, but I had prayed for provision so I would not get hit in the spine by an excited fan. God's watchful eye was on every detail of my day. I realized that I had never understood the depth of His love for me. The more He pours into me, the more I realize I am deficient in my understanding of love's power.

When weighing the risks versus benefits, we may be presented with an opportunity to enjoy the journey. God's Word admonishes: "Casting the whole of your care *[all your anxieties, all your worries, all your concerns, once and for all] on Him, for He cares for you affectionately and cares about you watchfully*" (1 Pet. 5:7). With this in mind, ask yourself:

1. What is my understanding of this powerful principle?

2. What is my understanding of the difference between identifying and expressing my feelings versus walking in the spirit of peace, joy, and self-control? What is my most common avenue/method of expression of my feelings? Am I patient with myself, allowing His grace to develop the fruits of the Spirit within me?

Chapter 9

THE POWER OF LOVE: RESTORATION AND LIFE

He who dwells in the secret place of the Most High
shall remain stable and fixed under the shadow of the
Almighty [Whose power no foe can withstand]. I will
say of the Lord, He is my Refuge and my Fortress, my
God; on Him I lean and rely, and in Him I [confidently]
trust!...He shall call upon Me, and I will answer
him; I will be with him in trouble, I will deliver him
and honor him. With long life will I satisfy him and
show him My salvation (Psalm 91:1-2;15-16).

THE WEEK AFTER RETURNING HOME FROM THE FOOTBALL GAME
in 2009, I was weak and exhausted. While attempting to make
homemade meat pie for my family's dinner, I ended up with a setback in my legs and hip. Walking became a chore even with the
cane, and I soon requested that my walker be brought up from the

basement. In what can only be described as perfect, providential timing, Carmen came to me the following week with wonderful news from Julie, one of my dearest friends in leadership at church. Julie informed Carmen that, after months of planning, a group of women arranged for a temporary stair lift to be put on the main staircase leading to my bedroom. I was shocked that anyone would give herself to such an effort, as I had never spoken with Julie about a stair lift. She is a woman of great stature in my eyes, and her grace and maturity are an example to the Body. Her life is evidence of one that produces much fruit, and though we rarely have time to be with one another, our hearts are knit closely. At first, I was afraid to accept such a gift and nervous about giving in to the pain in my legs. Surely, the chemotherapy would have an effect on the cancer in the bone, and we would not need any assistance.

The next morning, I listened to the Bible on CD as always. Ephesians 1:18,23 spoke to me in a powerful way:

> *By having the eyes of your heart flooded with light, so that you can know and understand the hope to which He has called you, and how rich is His glorious inheritance in the saints (His set-apart ones)…Which is His body, the fullness of Him Who fills all in all [for in that body lives the full measure of Him Who makes everything complete, and Who fills everything everywhere with Himself].*

In my mind and heart, I could never be good enough for my healing. But the Lord continued to work a miracle in my spirit by healing the pointless shame I carried over accepting gifts that were not "earned" in any way. The shame was buried deep, and opening up the wound to clean it was very painful. As the Body of Christ continued to pour generously into my life, part of me kept praying,

"Okay, Lord, you can stop now before this gets embarrassing! After all, what will people begin to say?" Memories of the trauma from the estrangement with my family flooded my mind. Being diagnosed with a rare form of cancer (that at the time was unfamiliar to most of the medical community) resulted in hesitancy from my family to offer the support needed as I came out of shock. Proverbs 27:4 states, "...*who is able to stand before jealousy?*" The brokenness and jealousy in the spirit of one of my sisters brought a tornado of confusion at the time of my diagnosis in 1994.

What began as fundraising support from my work community ended in shame, lies, and a stripping of all I knew and held dear. Wreaking havoc upon my extended family, she mockingly proclaimed, "Nothing serious is wrong with Laura." My sister called the young widows support group that was spearheading the fundraiser and threatened to sue them if support for the fundraiser was given. She told them my decision to seek a treatment aimed at keeping me in remission (the myeloma was slow-growing at that time) was not supported by the family. She fully believed and expressed her opinion that myeloma only strikes its victims after the age of eighty and that I was *surely* exaggerating my need for treatment! In this season, however, the Great Redeemer had plans for the healing of my soul. Shame was nailed to the cross, along with multiple myeloma!

When a family member operates in chaos and dysfunction, it is primarily important to identify what behavior is detrimental to the relationship and to our own emotional and spiritual well-being. Often, mindsets about the issue are based upon "opinions" that stem from unhealthy motives. Confrontation of the behavior and establishment of boundaries in the relationship are vitally important to personal breakthrough in a situation similar to mine. Regarding relationships, Amos 3:3 offers this counsel: *"Do two walk together except they make an appointment and have agreed?"* This question is not a command to think alike in all matters, but an exhortation to purify our hearts by seeking understanding of the pain inflicted, paired with a desire for restoration through restitution. Taking a time of separation from the relationship to rebuild trust may be necessary. On that note, we must avoid the pressure to simply "keep the peace" and quickly head back into relationship with the offender. Without taking time for issues to be dealt with and repentance to manifest, we are setting ourselves up for the repeated cycle of behavior that initially caused the breach.

Choosing an appropriate and timely response to the matter is found through honest and open prayer before the Lord, through regular study in the Word, and through qualified and experienced counsel. Through godly counsel, one is empowered to identify and deal with the unhealthy and dysfunctional family behavior patterns that fueled a relationship dynamic like the one I just described. Many years later, my sister regretted her actions and asked for forgiveness. Seeking restoration, she came to my assistance in the midst of my treatment.

I wrote a note to one of our pastors, Jeanne, sharing my feelings of vulnerability. The Holy Spirit then reminded me of two words that were prophesied to Jerry and me in recent years. The first one was given to my husband while praying for me: "Laura, you have hidden in the crowd long enough! In the days ahead, the Lord is going to call you forth, and you will be seen and no longer hidden." The Lord then affirmed this message through Pastor Loren, who prophesied over us stating, "Because you asked for wisdom and not riches, like Solomon, I will bless you." Little did I know what that blessing would look like in the days ahead! Over and over again, the Lord graciously poured His graces upon us, with repeated prophetic encouragement confirming His provision. This continual outpouring prepared me to receive God's gracious gifts, even though the "old" Laura kept looking over her shoulder to see if anyone was watching with a critical eye!

Jeanne finally said to me a month later, "Laura, just be who you are!" I realized then that I must continue to look forward and press on for wholeness and healing! Though the journey looks very different than I ever anticipated, the promise is a by-product of the love the Father has for me, and I graciously received the words that Pastor Loren prayed over me during our midweek service: "The former things are gone; I speak resurrection life over her!"

As each day passed, I clung to the message of life and kept hearing in my spirit, "I am your exceeding and great reward!" Pastor Rich confirmed this word the following month during our church's prayer service for the nations. He shared what the Lord had spoken to him: "What is impossible with man is possible with God, Laura. He is your exceeding and great reward, aside from the gifts and blessings He bestows." I pondered these things in my heart.

The faithful words of my shepherds were like a balm for my physical, emotional, and spiritual well-being. In turn, the Lord continually spoke to me regarding the anointing in His people, namely, a word He was giving me for Pastor Loren. The Lord reminded me that it was the "anointing that breaks every yoke." He spoke to me about the faithfulness of our pastor, who always keeps his gentle hand on the pulse of his sheep, which is the heart of Christ. The Lord recalled how Loren "had been faithful with little, so I will make him ruler over much..."

It was encouraging when Pastor Loren's message the next day confirmed this word. Loren reminded the congregation that the anointing is the Spirit of Christ within us and most important is the stewardship over everything God has placed in our hands and has called us to be. With every breath I took during his message, my heart cried for more and more wisdom and understanding as I walk out this journey.

The Lord's leading continued to be revealed at this time, and He had a strong message for my husband, as well. At our prophetic prayer meeting, Jerry spoke about authority and walking in the realm of the Kingdom and not the realm of our own reasoning. Shortly after, one of the ministers prayed for my husband and spoke to him, declaring that God was indeed giving Jerry authority and would show him many things in the days ahead about walking in that place. He then encouraged Jerry to begin taking authority over my illness.

Two weeks later, Barry and Krisanna, our spiritual son and daughter, came for a visit, and Jerry shared how much the word regarding our God-given authority had ministered to him. The Lord showed my husband that he (Jerry) had allowed our circumstances, specifically my illness, to "rule over" him, placing him in a subservient role to it. Continuing to explain what had been revealed, Jerry shared that the Lord then commanded him to take authority over my illness and no longer give the disease that place over him. Instead, the authority from the Father would rule over my illness! How patient is the Lord as He guides us into all righteousness and truth!

I could see the energy and life in Jerry's face as he spoke this revelation, and it confirmed for me that the presence of the Lord is the key to victory in all things! All wisdom, healing, and deliverance come from Him, but He truly is the greatest reward as we are changed by the transformation of our old nature—a resurrection to new life! Oh that we would see with His eyes, hear with His ears, think with His mind, and feel what His heart feels! Seeking after these things is truly "working out our salvation with fear and trembling" (see Phil. 2:12). Is this not the fear of the Lord, which is the beginning of wisdom?

My home looked beautiful for Thanksgiving—the result of the work of many helping hands. A group of ladies in the church came as a surprise and decorated with Jerry's help so that our grandchildren could enjoy the Christmas tree, and we were able to invite some of our church family members who did not have a place to celebrate. Though I was tired, I stepped into my place as mother when it was time to serve the meal. Everything was delicious, and our time together was full of joy! Again, the holiday had the signature of God's love written all over it. Though different, He restored more to me than I had the year before.

Our Christmas holidays were going to be very special as my dear friend, Mary Anne, invited our family to stay at her New York City apartment over the holiday break. It had been fifteen years since my diagnosis in 1994, and we had not had a vacation with our children since that time. Immediately, we began researching restaurants and making reservations for the trip.

We knew the holidays were going to be busy in the city, and we wanted to make certain things would run as smoothly as possible so I would not have to stand in lines or risk injury to my back. After celebrating Christmas Eve together and attending our church candlelight service, we spent Christmas Day packing and left early the next morning for the airport.

Although Jerry and I were a bit nervous about the trip, given my condition, we knew God had planned the whole thing, so we went forward in trust. God had already made a way: for two weeks before we departed, I was able to stop using my cane! With anticipation of His wonderful provision, we prayed together before boarding our flight. Just the day before, there had been a failed terrorist bombing attempt on a flight landing at the Detroit airport, so we knew security would be on high alert. As we prayed, the Holy Spirit spoke to my heart and said, "The blessing of the Lord brings wealth, and He adds no trouble to it." His peace poured over me like warm oil, and from that moment I was at rest.

Our son-in-law, Bryan, obtained tickets for our family to see the Radio City Music Hall Christmas Extravaganza along with a Broadway play, and we were excited to take in the sights and sounds of the city. Since I had scheduled an appointment with Dr. Gonzalez at his New York City office later in the week, the kids planned to leave and travel back to Detroit ahead of us. It would be a long stay for us, but every minute was wonderful and filled with fun. Jerry was able to relax and enjoy my company, stepping out of his role as caregiver, since there was always another pair of eyes watching me and an extra set of arms supporting me while we moved about the city.

Dear friends joined us in the city the day the kids left to return home. Before the kids departed, they treated our family to brunch, and we all gathered in Mary Anne's living room to pray.

Jerry began to weep and asked for help to start the prayer so he could gather himself. Our friends sensitively knew how to pray at that moment, thanking the Lord for our time together. Although Jerry continued to weep, he gained enough composure to pray through his tears, and the kids were able to see his heart as he expressed the heart of God for all of them.

My appointment with Dr. Gonzalez showed good results with some stress evident on my organs from the chemotherapy. Dr. Gonzalez, like my oncologist, reported excellent bone marrow scores and a strong hemoglobin count of 14.5! This was not only good for a woman's hemoglobin, but it was considered an excellent score for a man. The doctor shook his head in disbelief, confounded by the fact that my bone marrow was producing great blood cells even though there was metastasis to the bone. I pondered that fact with the Lord in prayer for days after I returned home. He spoke to me and reminded me of a prophetic word I had received many years ago: "You have royal blood running through your veins, daughter, and when the doctors have done all they can do, I will give you a transfusion from My throne!" Truly, His miraculous power was in motion, and He again spoke to me and said, "My life is in the blood, Laura." Oh, the precious blood of Jesus and its power to heal and deliver! That word would again try me in the days ahead, and I would cling to it with every ounce of my being!

To this day, we continue to talk about our trip to New York City with great fondness. Jerry, who had been the most apprehensive about spending ten days in the city, had the best time of all. We cannot wait to spend time with our children again and make more memories together. Our trip reinforced the importance of time spent with loved ones—time for precious communion with one another—and the power of love to restore and breathe life into our circumstances.

I approached the new year with renewed fervor for getting back into shape, so I carefully began using exercise bands and walking each day. What began as a two-minute walk quickly became thirty minutes daily by the end of January! I was so excited, but I soon noticed some back pain and difficulty rising from a chair without help. *Why, Lord, does it seem that I take one step forward, only to take two steps back?* The pain was all too familiar, so I asked the doctor's assistant to schedule an MRI of the spine and pelvis to rule out a vertebral fracture. The nerve affected by the lesion on my sacral spine was hurting badly, and the pain shot across my pelvic bones and around my waist. Every day that passed brought more severe pain, and again I needed Oxycontin and Oxycodone in order to function. Could it be that my choice to do oral chemotherapy was not working and the cancer was spreading? I cried out to the Lord for answers, and He reminded me of a word given to me by Pastor Loren at our Thanksgiving Eve service: "The former has gone; resurrection life do I declare." I needed to trust that word!

The initial results of my MRI indicated changes to my status, so my oncologist immediately scheduled a meeting to review my treatment plan. I prayed and left a message that I would meet with him after he reviewed all of my most recent tests against the MRI, knowing that the facility reporting the changes was only comparing the MRI results with those on file from a test the previous year. I did not want any faulty conclusions drawn, as it was crucial to view the most recent PET scan done in August, just six months earlier, which revealed lesions in my arm, thighs, pelvis, and sacral spine.

The oncologist reviewed my MRI report against the PET scan, along with all MRI results from the past two years. Much to his surprise, my bones showed improvement, so there was relief that the chemotherapy was working. It was decided that I would see my neurosurgeon to get his opinion on the vertebrae with the lesion and to discuss possible nerve involvement given the severity of the pain I was experiencing. With his guidance, we would determine if physical therapy alone was sufficient to bring relief, or if I would need to add radiation to my treatment plan. One thing I knew for certain: I could not live in the pain I was experiencing, and I deeply desired to return to normal activity.

Though frustrated and battle weary, I continued to fight for each step toward healing, even though there seemed to be a constant barrier at every turn. The battle wore on, bringing repeated rounds of dying to self physically. I gained weight from the Dexamethasone, a steroid which was added to my chemotherapy protocol. The steroid had many side effects, including thinning of the bones, so the forty-five extra pounds it added to my osteoporotic skeletal structure did not help my attitude toward the drug. With Doc's permission, I began to slowly wean off my weekly dosage of the steroid, while hoping to make progress with the Revlimid alone. In prayer, I asked the Lord to cover me, believing I was in the season of my healing.

I grieved the loss of mental alertness caused by the use of narcotics for pain, and I dreaded the withdrawal symptoms that would surely come when it was time to wean off of them. Having been down that road before, I had no desire to relive the experience. I needed the pain medication to function from day to day, but when I wanted to be in prayer and have the most concentration, I was unable to do so according to my hopes. Again, I had to lean on the grace of the Father to cover me and hear the cry of my heart within, even though it was difficult to pray with eloquence and order. "'...*Not by might, nor by power, but by My Spirit,' says the Lord...*" (Zech. 4:6 NIV). I am reminded daily that my desire to have all of Him indeed pleases Him. Each hour is a constant leaning upon Him for all of my strength.

A few weeks after returning home from our vacation in New York, I did as my oncologist recommended and made an appointment with my neurosurgeon. He reviewed the films and ordered a bone scan of my entire body to determine if he could help in any way. If the scan revealed a fracture, a kyphoplasty would be in order to repair the vertebrae with "bone cement." The results indicated that there was indeed a fracture at T-11, along with several rib fractures and blastic lesions from my feet up to my skull. My neurosurgeon, radiation oncologist, and my oncologist all agreed that I.V. chemotherapy was needed after surgery. Velcade was the drug of choice since I had not used it in over three years. Given the condition of my skeletal structure, the Revlimid was obviously not working, so the oral drug Thalidomide was prescribed—the only choice left under the circumstances.

Knowing the urgency of the situation and the tenuous condition of my spine, my neurosurgeon squeezed me into his schedule before leaving on vacation, thus avoiding any delay in my chemotherapy plan. The surgery went as smoothly as possible, and the kyphoplasty relieved my nerve pain and gave my spine more stability. Another bone marrow biopsy was also in order, but the first attempt failed and a repeat was scheduled right away. The final procedure was the reinsertion of a port, something I fought against for a long time. I wept intensely, feeling as though I was again stepping into a world of which I wanted no part. I did not like the loss of freedom caused by I.V. chemotherapy, nor did I welcome the added risk of port infections, which always resulted in hospitalization. Between the surgery, biopsies, and other procedures, I was at the hospital more than I ever wanted to be within a three-week period. Hospitalizations are always a traumatic time, causing both physical and emotional stress and strain.

When it appeared as though the trauma could not increase, 2011 proved to be a nightmare. After the holidays, Carmen noticed a bulging from my right thigh. Using a walker, I was unable to navigate and became bedbound with unbearable pain. Insisting I go for x-rays, Carmen and her boyfriend, Jamal, took me to a nearby clinic for tests. Jamal, who has been unshakeable in his support, accompanied Carmen and me to most of my appointments that year.

When I arrived at my oncologist's office for results, the doctor walked in the room and informed me that the noticeable bulge in my thigh was, in fact, the femoral head, which had rotated and then healed in the wrong direction due to a break in my femur. Because of the risk of infection and paralysis, I was hospitalized immediately. After four days of testing and evaluation at one hospital, I was transported by ambulance to a larger medical center for surgery as my case was referred to one of the top orthopedic oncologists in the state. My experience under her care, though painful, was most rewarding. Dr. Les respected the sensitivity of my situation and gave serious consideration to my input at every turn, always leaving me with the sense that I was in control.

Since the orthopedic and trauma surgeons agreed that my bones were not capable of holding pins due to severe decomposition, Dr. Les concurred with my husband's research that a replacement of my femur and right hip socket was necessary. Surgery was scheduled for the following morning. The surgical prep team was kind and supportive, and they were sensitive in allowing my family to meet the anesthesiologist and nurses who would be involved in the operating room. We all were at peace, hopeful that there would be an end to my year of confinement in bed.

I worked diligently to regain my strength after the surgery so that I could be discharged as soon as possible and continue therapy at home. Before I left the hospital, Dr. Les advised that she was concerned about a spot on my spine, so further testing was ordered after my discharge. As always, my physical symptoms indicated that something was seriously wrong, and I waited anxiously for the results. After only three weeks at home, I received a call from Dr. Les, and she informed me that I needed to return to the hospital as results indicated another tumor on my spine, which was the size of a baseball. The pain was increasing hour by hour, and by the time we were prepared to leave home yet again, the pain was so intense that Jerry had to call an ambulance. My groans turned to screaming, and the kids immediately called Melissa home to accompany them to the hospital; they needed her support and encouragement.

Panicked by all that was happening, Jerry slipped and fell down the stairs and broke his ankle while calling for emergency assistance. The weight of this "cross" had clearly become too heavy to bear in that moment. But even our Lord and Savior fell under the weight of His cross, and even He accepted the help of a mere passerby. Why should we expect anything different of our loved ones and ourselves when the road becomes unbearable? Those of us who are strong in the moment are called to wrap our hands around the "wood" and shoulder the burden for those who are weak. This was certainly a lesson that my family was learning and living each and every day.

Needless to say, Jerry and I were quite a pair as I arrived at the hospital on a gurney and he in a wheelchair pushed by Carmen's boyfriend, Jamal! The surgery lasted long into the evening, leaving me in intensive care in the middle of the night. Jerry and the kids sat many hours in the surgical waiting room, praying and holding on to the knowledge that God would accomplish all He had promised on this journey. Weary from watching me suffer, their faith and the support of friends and family sustained them.

The procedure was lengthy, and I lost a large quantity of blood as the spinal surgeon removed a bleeding plasma cytoma from my lower spine and added titanium rods to my spinal column. My postsurgical stay was difficult as blood transfusions left me reacting with convulsive fevers and difficulty breathing. I started physical therapy right away to regain movement, but because of my recent femur replacement, the hospital staff recommended placement in a rehabilitation unit. Since my family understood the emotional impact of a transfer to a nursing home facility, they requested the rehab unit at the hospital.

Jerry and the kids tried to ease the trauma of being separated from them for what seemed like an eternity away from home. Nevertheless, I sank into depression. Since the beginning of this phase of my battle with cancer in 2006, I had not experienced despair to this intensity, and my weeping turned to wailing. My sisters took turns staying with me so I would not be left alone, and Carmen regularly participated in my therapy protocol. I could see the deep concern in their faces. The increasing severity of my situation was sinking in, and the uncertain road ahead left each one of us clinging desperately to hope.

Each time it seemed as though we were able to come up out of the water to catch our breath, a tsunami was again on the horizon, crashing over our lives and leaving us battle weary. Without any time to recover, I was hospitalized twice more for port infections through the end of March of that year (2011). Sensing a heavy despair in my spirit, my nurse practitioner, Suzanne, provided information on post-traumatic stress disorder, which is experienced by many cancer patients—40 percent of all cases. This information helped me understand and validate my experience, including the horrifying flashbacks that lasted for one year and still occur on occasion.

My heart aches for the terminally ill and others who have to remain hospitalized for an extended period. The loneliness and deep longing for the comforts of home, combined with the fear of further medical complications, can cause a sense of dark despair, even in the hearts of the most faithful. I praise God for the Body of Christ, for my loved ones have helped sustain me through one hospitalization after another. While I understand the importance of prudent medical care in the proper time, the foundation of my faith and expectation is that the Lord is my Healer. Medical reports may present facts; however, the present, active, and living truth of the Word of God supersedes fact, and *that* Truth boldly pronounces that "...*with the stripes [that wounded] Him we are healed and made whole*" (Isa. 53:5).

As I end this chapter, I'd like you to take a moment to reflect upon the principles I shared in describing the relationship turmoil I faced at the onset of my diagnosis. As you think about the relationships in your own life, ask yourself the following questions:

1. When I am in a strenuous relationship situation where confrontation and course-adjustment are necessary, what personal

motivations fuel my choice of counsel? Do I seek guidance from a seasoned, godly leader (such as a counselor or pastor) who might challenge my own mindsets concerning the situation, or do I prioritize my comfort by only sharing with peers who might not be equipped to help me deal with the core issue(s) at hand?

2. Which of my thoughts, emotions, and behaviors reveal foundations in unhealthy mindsets or beliefs that are not in line with my true identity in Christ?

Chapter 10

DAWNING OF A NEW DAY

Truly I tell you, whoever says to this mountain, Be
lifted up and thrown into the sea! and does not doubt
at all in his heart but believes that what he says will
take place, it will be done for him. For this reason
I am telling you, whatever you ask for in prayer,
believe (trust and be confident) *that it is granted*
to you, and you will [get it] (Mark 11:23-24).

WHEN I BEGAN TO WRITE THIS BOOK, I ASKED THE LORD WHAT
He wanted me to title it. The Holy Spirit immediately brought
to my remembrance a prophetic word given to me at a Women's
Aglow meeting in 1995. The speaker gave her testimony, and I
was amazed by the similarities of our paths. I was at a very dark
place in my life, having just been diagnosed with cancer, displaced
from the home that I loved, and estranged in some of my personal
relationships. Much to my surprise, the speaker pointed to me
and requested that I come forward. She wrapped her arms around

me and whispered in my ear about the love the Father has for me. I could not grasp the love she described, and little did I know the road that lay ahead. Speaking to me with quiet confidence, she proclaimed, "Daughter, you have been called to a dark road, but you will be victorious!"

In all honesty, there have been days throughout the years of this journey when it has been very difficult to hold fast to the hope of victory. It's in these moments that I have had to realign my heart to His Word and His promises and refocus my affection for His presence. When affliction or disease is present in a person's life, emotional vulnerability is a prime catalyst the enemy uses to speak lies of reproach, condemnation, fear, and shame. Thoughts like *I'm not desirable to be around* and *I'm too much of a burden for everyone* can run rampant in the mind, causing us to lose our peace and hope. When these assaults come my way, the Lord is always faithful to surround and shield me with acceptance, affirmation, and love. There are days when our home is filled with visitors, and they often worry that they are bothering us. However, we are always comforted by the presence of those who are sent with a purpose. It seems our loved ones know what they are meant to impart and always allow us to gauge what we are able to receive.

For a season (during the summer of 2011), my dear friend, Holly, came and helped prepare meals each week. This was a blessing since I had lost over forty pounds and was having difficulty keeping my meals down. During her visits, Holly prayed quietly as she faithfully rubbed my feet. She knew that my feet ached and always carefully massaged my legs, checking for dehydration, blood clots, and atrophy. One evening in particular, it was quite late when we heard the door open and footsteps come toward the kitchen. It was Holly, and the Lord had directed her to come. As she entered the room, I was vomiting once again. Without wavering, Holly checked me for thrush and helped me call the doctor for a prescription. Intending to send Carmen to the pharmacy the next morning, I thanked Holly for her tender care as she headed home. Within the hour, however, Holly was back at our door, medication in hand. To this day, she continues to pour her gifts into my life, and I am grateful for her kindness.

Every day, I must choose to rise above the depression and the fear of cancer consuming my body. During the large amount of time I have to ponder and pray, the Lord revealed a broken place within me that came forth after facing the reality of some of my relationships. Suffering has a way of unearthing things that have been hidden in darkness, and my dear friend, Julie, helped me grapple with them. She tiptoed with grace upon my heart, always bringing a word of life just when it seemed I could barely climb out of the dark tunnel of illness, pain, and hopelessness. It is in these moments of darkness that the prayers of my son, Christopher, are so precious to me! He prays for me daily, filling me with encouragement from God's Word, declaring healing over my body. If my speech turns negative, he corrects it immediately with loving patience.

God's Word is living and active in our home. Melissa, Christopher, and Carmen grow daily in wisdom and stature, each one passing the baton to the other while supporting Jerry and me. As parents, we remain a steady force in the lives of our children. Yet, throughout the journey, our young adult children have reciprocated with the same level of steadfast support. With each passing day, Jerry and I are blessed to witness the awesome fruit of the training of the Holy Spirit in the lives of our children.

My dear husband, Jerry, remains forever loyal and steady. As we continue the journey together, I know that he will keep one hand in mine while the other points the way to new possibilities, hopes, and dreams. The relationship he maintains in the Secret Place of the Most High God sheds light upon God's predictability. During incredible stress and feelings of uncertainty, our love for Jesus Christ and one another always breathes life and hope into our hearts.

When the side effects of the drugs and treatment make perseverance appear difficult, I have to make an active decision to *choose life*. Grappling with such profound issues keeps me reaching out to my loved ones and to the Lord. In moments of vulnerable transparency, I weep more often, allowing my family and friends to speak into my spirit. My sisters are prayer warriors with me, standing *without compromise* for a miracle. They call, visit, and e-mail their prayers for me. When my sister, Elvie, phones from many miles away, she offers encouraging words, even as we weep together. Another sister, Barbara, calls often to tell me she loves me and once shared a revelation she received, which unveiled an overwhelming sense of my healing and a vision of me standing on my own. Oh, how I desire to shed this walker and run again! As the Lord continues to remind me, healing often comes as a seed, and line upon line, the manifestation becomes apparent.

Many have helped nurture the seed of healing with tender, loving hands, and it seems that a deep work is being done in all of us.

Even while I am struggling physically, the light of revelation within me burns brighter. No matter how serious my prognosis, every ounce of concern melts away with excitement over the dawning of a new day in God's Kingdom. Our Savior came to make known the Father and shed light on the truths of His Kingdom. Of Him, John 1:9 says, *"That was the true Light which gives light to every man coming into the world"* (NKJV). In response, we are called to spread His light, for in Proverbs 4:18 we are told, *"But the path of the just is like the shining sun, that shines ever brighter unto the perfect day"* (NKJV).

Longing to bask in and share the Lord's radiance with my church family, I wait each Wednesday evening for Christopher to come home with a recording of the service. My pastor's message always brings me comfort, and the flame within me cannot be quenched. The sons of God will be revealed in the earth, and those who prepare their hearts and lives will be the first fruits to manifest God's glory. Again, I reflect on the promise in Proverbs: *"But the path of the just is like the shining sun, that shines ever brighter unto the perfect day"* (Prov. 4:18 NKJV). God is calling a people out of a people who will walk in His light, which is our life! The Kingdom is at hand (see Matt. 10:7) and within each of us (see Luke 17:21). As such, the power and authority to overcome sickness, sin, and bondage has been made available to us!

The Holy Spirit reminds me daily of words that have been spoken over my life. My pastor prayed for me as I entered this last battle, proclaiming, "The enemy has come to defeat you in this season, but you will defeat every giant that comes against you." The Lord repeatedly reminds me that perfect love casts out fear! When we fight in the dark, everything appears bigger and scarier than it is in reality. The Lord placed a burden on my heart, revealing that I must look toward the light to fight this battle. As I turn toward the light, the sun begins to rise, and everything is seen more clearly. The Scriptures tell us that when Joshua and Caleb were in battle, they looked toward the light. Once they did so, they knew they could defeat the enemy! That same promise is true for you and for me: turning toward the Light enables us to overcome any challenge and defeat any foe in battle.

The Light of Christ came to reveal the hearts of people. Once that truth comes forth, the opportunity for choice exists. Each season brings a greater revelation of His nature through His Body—the Church. Jesus is coming for a Bride without spot, wrinkle, or blemish (see Eph. 5:27). This is a light and reality revealed, not hidden. Light and love are transparent, honest, and without hidden agendas. *Oh Lord, let us surrender ourselves, dying to our flesh completely, that we might turn from the ways of man and inherit a share in Your divine life. Your Kingdom come on earth as it is in Heaven!*

Years ago, one of the ministers from our church, Ruben, spoke with me about the meat of God's Word made transparent and available through our family. Again, his message was a foreshadowing of things to come! Every time the Lord brings a servant spirit—a precious caregiver for my family and me—Jerry and I know it is never just about us. Each one enters our home and is changed. One by one, they are exposed to greater light and life through the gifts we freely offer. Never did I anticipate that those who are sent to care for us during our devastation would receive an outpouring of wisdom, counsel, and love; but God's ways are not our ways!

God is not the author of sickness and disease. He does not bring disease upon His people to teach us lessons or "make us more mature." He is good, loving, and merciful! Even if we do face physical illness or disease, it is never an unredeemable situation. God promises to work *all things* together for our benefit (see Rom. 8:28). As He did with Joseph in the Old Testament, our Father will take what is meant for evil and use it for good. In a lost and dying world, we, His Church, will serve to advance the Kingdom as we walk with Him.

I want to encourage you to see yourself not through the lens of your circumstances, but through the lens of Father's love, which casts out all fear and every tormenting thought (see 1 John 4:18). His thoughts and plans for your life are great (see Jer. 29:11). You may be facing sickness, but your identity is not in that disease. Healing is yours in Jesus' name! You may have experienced rejection by those closest to you, but you are not a castaway! You may have even made very poor choices throughout life, but today is a new day to receive forgiveness and start fresh through the redemptive power of the blood of Jesus. It's time to start seeing yourself as God sees you and to declare His Word over your own life. As you do so, ask yourself the following:

1. What does the Word say about my present circumstance? Have I received prophetic words that speak to my identity in Christ and to my purpose in Him?

2. Take time to invest in this exercise. Write down your findings and keep them accessible

throughout the day; meditate on them and declare them out loud.

3. Who are some of the most trusted and valuable people in my life who will not only encourage me and remind me of what God has said concerning my life, but will hold me accountable to staying on course, especially when difficult circumstances threaten to distract me from pressing into the Lord for victory?

As Jesus carried the cross down the Via Dolorosa, every step toward His destiny destroyed satan's plan, making provision for us, His people, to share in the richness of the Kingdom as sons and daughters of the Most High. This authority was meant for us from the beginning. Because of His death and resurrection, the provision for the healing of our bodies and the destruction of sickness and disease was made available to us. Because of His great love, the Holy Spirit—the very Spirit of Christ—dwells in each of us. He illuminates even the darkest road so that we, His Body, will walk in power and authority, destroying the works of the devil and demonstrating that the Kingdom is indeed at hand!

As the Bible declares:

For with God nothing is ever impossible and no word from God shall be without power or impossible of fulfillment (Luke 1:37).

ABOUT LAURA KYMLA

LauraKymla.com

info@LauraKymla.com

Find Laura on Facebook and @LauraKymla on Twitter

IN THE RIGHT HANDS, THIS BOOK WILL CHANGE LIVES!

Most of the people who need this message will not be looking for this book. To change their lives, you need to put a copy of this book in their hands.

> *But others (seeds) fell into good ground, and brought forth fruit, some a hundred-fold, some sixty-fold, some thirty-fold* (Matthew 13:8).

Our ministry is constantly seeking methods to find the good ground, the people who need this anointed message to change their lives. Will you help us reach these people?

> *Remember this—a farmer who plants only a few seeds will get a small crop. But the one who plants generously will get a generous crop* (2 Corinthians 9:6).

**EXTEND THIS MINISTRY BY SOWING
3 BOOKS, 5 BOOKS, 10 BOOKS, OR MORE TODAY,
AND BECOME A LIFE CHANGER!**

Thank you,

Don Nori Sr., Founder
Destiny Image
Since 1982

DESTINY IMAGE PUBLISHERS, INC.

"Promoting Inspired Lives."

VISIT OUR NEW SITE HOME AT
WWW.DESTINYIMAGE.COM

FREE SUBSCRIPTION TO DI NEWSLETTER

Receive free unpublished articles by top DI authors, exclusive

discounts, and free downloads from our best and newest books.

Visit www.destinyimage.com to subscribe.

Write to: Destiny Image
                     P.O. Box 310
                     Shippensburg, PA 17257-0310

Call: 1-800-722-6774

Email: orders@destinyimage.com

For a complete list of our titles or to place an order
online, visit www.destinyimage.com.

FIND US ON FACEBOOK OR FOLLOW US ON TWITTER.

www.facebook.com/destinyimage   facebook
www.twitter.com/destinyimage   twitter